TWAYNE'S WORLD AUTHORS SERIES

A Survey of the World's Literature

FRANCE

Maxwell A. Smith, Guerry Professor of French, Emeritus
The University of Chattanooga
Former Visiting Professor in Modern Languages
The Florida State University
EDITOR

Eugène Scribe

TWAS 547

Eugène Scribe

EUGÈNE SCRIBE

By HELENE KOON
and RICHARD SWITZER

*California State College,
San Bernardino*

TWAYNE PUBLISHERS

A DIVISION OF G. K. HALL & CO., BOSTON

Published in 1980 by Twayne Publishers,
A Division of G. K. Hall & Co.
All Rights Reserved

Printed on permanent/durable acid-free paper and bound
in the United States of America

First Printing

Frontispiece of Eugène Scribe
is an engraved rendering
of a photograph by Nadar

Library of Congress Cataloging in Publication Data

Koon, Helene, 1925 -
Eugène Scribe.

(Twayne's world authors series ; TWAS 547 : France)
Bibliography: p. 166 - 68
Includes index.
1. Scribe, Augustin Eugène, 1791 - 1861—
Criticism and interpretation. I. Switzer, Richard, joint author.
PQ2425.Z5K6   842'.7   78-31370
ISBN 0-8057-6390-2

Contents

About the Authors

Preface

Chronology

1. The Life and Times of Eugène Scribe   11

2. Scribe and His Stage Technique   35

3. The Social Comedies   61

4. The History Plays   86

5. Scribe's Influence   111

6. Scribe and Music   122

7. Conclusion   154

Notes and References   159

Selected Bibliography   166

Index   169

About the Authors

Helene Wickham Koon was born in Minneapolis, Minnesota. She holds advanced degrees from the Pasadena Playhouse and the University of California at Los Angeles, and is at present Professor of English and Chair of the English department at California State College, San Bernardino. For a number of years she worked in the theatre as actress, director and producer. Her poems and translations have been published in *Modern Images, Contrasts* and *The Journals of Pierre Menard*. She has edited *A Letter from Mr. Cibber to Mr. Pope* (1973) and, with Mary Mahl, *The Female Spectator: English Women Writers before 1800* (1977). Her article, "Pope's First Editors" appeared in the *Huntington Library Quarterly* (November, 1971) and on "Eliza Haywood and the Female Spectator" in the same journal (November, 1978). She has contributed to *The Reader's Encyclopedia of English Literature* (1976) and the *Guide to American Women Writers* (1978). She is presently engaged in research for a biography of Colley Cibber.

Richard Switzer studied French at the University of Chicago, the University of Nancy, the University of Paris, and the University of California (Berkeley), with a Ph.D. from the last institution. He has specialized in literature of the eighteenth and nineteenth centuries. He is the author of several books, editions, and translations of Chateaubriand (including the TWAS volume on Chateaubriand) and has published numerous articles in various journals. He has translated Scribe's *Glass of Water* for performance. He is currently Professor of French at California State College, San Bernardino; where he was Dean of Humanities until 1979; he taught previously at Wisconsin (Madison) where he was Professor of French and Chairman of the Department of French and Italiàn, and before that at Northwestern University.

Preface

Thanks to much of the criticism of Scribe written both by his contemporaries and by succeeding generations, Eugène Scribe is a much misunderstood author. Accustomed to a history of dramatic authors who were great literary figures, such as Corneille, Racine and Voltaire, the French critics frequently rejected him as unworthy from a literary point of view. And indeed, Scribe's plays do not reveal their full potential from a casual reading. His plays were not designed to be read, as were those of his countryman Musset somewhat later. Scribe requires performance. Only from the complete theatrical experience can the audience appreciate fully the dramatic power of the author.

Added to this misestimation of Scribe, which is understandable, there is another reason for a distortion of his reputation: envy. Many critics and fellow playwrights simply could not forgive Scribe his success. Their own plays, which they naturally considered as greatly superior to Scribe's, were not given the same enthusiastic approval by the public. A kind of snobbishness, such as the attitude voiced later by Flaubert, decreed that anything that appealed to the great majority must by necessity be inferior.

The fact remains, however, that not only was Scribe able to please his contemporary public, but he influenced the theater of all of Europe, affecting authors such as Bernard Shaw and Ibsen. Finally, and this is the true test of a playwright's lasting value, he can charm a modern audience as surely as he did those of the nineteenth century, as is witnessed by the 1976 revival in Paris at the Comédie Française, to the acclaim of both critics and public of *Le Verre d'eau, The Glass of Water*. Those who persist in denigrating Scribe either have not troubled to read the plays, relying on the parroting of the outdated critics, or else have been unable to bring to the reading of the plays that extra measure of imagination which allows the reader to visualise the play as it might appear on the stage.

The name of Scribe is inevitably linked to the expression, "pièce bien faite," translated as the "well-made play." The concept loses something in translation: what good play is not "well-made"? An attempt to define this expression has led many critics astray.

When a Frenchman goes to his dairy store to buy a cheese, he asks for one that is "bien fait." He is not inquiring into the skill of the cheesemaker, but rather is seeking a cheese which has arrived at that moment of perfection in its development when it can be most savored. Timing is likewise an important element in the makeup of the well-made play: the action must develop with that precise and appropriate timing which brings about the necessary and desired (on the part of the audience) end, while maintaining the required logic and progression. In *The Glass of Water*, the appropriate *dénouement* is brought on as an absolute necessity, given the precise situation that Scribe has built up for the final scene. In a similar manner, in *Adrienne Lecouvreur*, when Bouillon brings home from the Institute a poison which he has been asked to analyze, we are, without our realizing it, being prepared for the poisoning which will form the climax of the story.

To this extent plot is important. But little attention should be given to the critics who claim Scribe's work is nothing but plot, with no characterization and no convictions. On the contrary, the plot elements exist only to provide situations in which the individuals can reveal their characters, and they often display Scribe's convictions.

Perhaps the works of Scribe most frequently revived today are the libretti which he wrote for the foremost composers of his time: Rossini, Verdi, Halévy, Meyerbeer, Auber. Here too the custom is to sneer at Scribe, but a careful examination of the libretti shows the same mastery of the form that is evident in the dramas. Too often the libretti have been examined only as if they were plays which happened to be set to music, an attitude which completely disregards the very particular requirements of this, a totally different genre.

This volume, after a background sketch of his life and career, will attempt to examine the various genres practiced by Scribe, and to evaluate them in the light of theatrical realities.

California State College
San Bernardino, California

HELENE KOON and
RICHARD SWITZER

Chronology

1791   Birth of Scribe
1807   Death of Scribe's mother
1810   Scribe's first play: *Le Prétendu sans le savoir*
1815   Scribe's first great success: *Une nuit de la Garde nationale*
1825   *La Dame blanche* (Boieldieu)
1828   *Le Comte Ory* (Rossini)
1830   *Fra Diavolo* (Auber)
1831   *Robert le Diable* (Meyerbeer)
1836   Scribe elected to the Académie Française
1839   Marriage
1840   *Le Verre d'eau*
1849   *Adrienne Lecouvreur*
1851   *Bataille de dames*
1861   Death of Scribe
1865   *L'Africaine* (Meyerbeer)

CHAPTER 1

The Life and Times of Eugène Scribe

I   The Early Years

AUGUSTIN-EUGÈNE Scribe was a true Parisian whose years began and ended in the City of Light. He was born December 24, 1791, the child of a silk merchant whose shop, le Chat Noir, stood at the corner of the Rue Saint-Denis and the Rue Trousse-Vache[1] near the church of Saint Roche. The neighborhood was *les Halles*, appropriate for the man whose life and work would represent the highest ideals of the bourgeoisie.

His early personal history is sketchy. He published no memoirs, and only the barest facts are recorded. The context is dramatic; before he was two, the Reign of Terror had flourished, and by his eighth birthday, First Consul Napoleon was reshaping the map of Europe. Political and international upheavals undoubtedly affected the foundations of society, but daily life had to continue, and his childhood was probably serene. His father, who died when the boy was an infant, left a modest fortune, and his mother apparently lived quietly, devoting herself to the child's upbringing.

Their relationship seems to have been harmonious. Not only are the bourgeois virtues of honesty, integrity, ambition and industry applauded in his work, but they were also an integral part of his personality. His portraits of women are usually sympathetic except where plot demands are otherwise; nowhere in his writing is the slightest suggestion of any resentment toward his maternal parent.

He attended the prestigious Collège de Sainte-Barbe and proved a brilliant student, winning first prize for his work at the conclusion of his academic career. In the custom of the day, the young "laureate" was crowned under the dome of the Académie Francaise, the laurels bestowed by the playwright, Vincent-Antoine Arnault.[2]

Such a promising scholar should become more than a tradesman,

11

his mother decided, and sent him to study with Louis-Ferdinand Bonnet, the astute lawyer famous for his brilliant defense of General Jean-Victor Moreau.[3] In republican France, the bar could be a step to the Chamber of Deputies or even greater heights, and Madame Scribe no doubt hoped Eugène would follow his mentor's illustrious career. Unfortunately, young Scribe had acquired less "respectable" tastes at Sainte-Barbe; he had discovered the theater. The dutiful son tried to obey his mother's wishes, but he had found the ruling passion of his life, and nothing else mattered.

In 1807, Madame Scribe died, leaving her fifteen-year-old boy in Bonnet's care, but any hope of a law career ended at this time. With the only restraining influence gone, Scribe, with his old classmate, Germain Delavigne, devoted every waking hour to the theater. In vain did Bonnet threaten and cajole his charge to concentrate on his neglected studies; Scribe's mind was firmly fixed on the stage. At last, in despair, Bonnet sent him to the promising lawyer, Dupin, but even he was unable to bring the recalcitrant into the fold.

Their concern was justified; respect for the theater had declined ever since the days of Molière. Except for the Comédie-Française (which also was suspect), the stage was seen to provide popular entertainment for the masses but certainly no career for a gifted intellectual. Under the Republic, there no longer existed hope for gaining reputation and position through court patronage; sober citizens regarded the boulevard theaters as at best a waste of time, at worst as dens of iniquity.

Young Scribe was not in the least concerned for the dreary respectability of a barrister's office. Fortunately, his economic circumstances allowed him a certain freedom; he was not rich, but because his inheritance was sufficient, he was under no compulsion to earn his living.[4] He not only continued to visit the theater, but, to his guardian's horror, began to write for it and soon put away his law books forever.

Bonnet may have feared that, like many young wastrels, Scribe was simply drawn by the glamour of the stage and the free behavior of its denizens. If so, he did not know his charge. Scribe was not at all interested in the demimonde of the playhouse world. By nature ambitious and by training strongly disciplined, he set about achieving his goal in the only way he knew—by way of industrious application. His work habits which were probably established at this time, would not vary throughout his life. He rose early, and by five A.M. was at the high desk where he stood and wrote until noon.

After a light lunch, he spent the rest of the day planning new work. Although he was a quiet man who avoided café life, he was not antisocial. An excellent host, every Thursday evening he was at home to friends. The theater was never out of his mind; a favorite game was played at the dinner table: one person thought of an idea, another plotted it, a third created the dialogue. The aim was to finish it by the end of the meal.[5]

II   *The First Plays*

In spite of such commitment, the reception given his early efforts was sufficient to discourage all but the most dedicated. His very first play, a one-act vaudeville. *Le Prétendu par hasard, ou l'Occasion fait le larron*, opened January 13, 1810 at the Variétés. Within minutes, the audience demonstrated its candid opinion with whistles, bursts of loud laughter and volleys of ironic applause until the curtain had to be dropped. Potier, one of the actors, came out to try and subdue the uproar while protecting the youthful playwright:

Gentlemen, the play we have just had the honor of presenting to you is the first attempt of a very young author. He recognizes the applause you would prefer to give him as a mark of encouragement and begs you will allow him to remain anonymous.[6]

Scribe had barely turned nineteen, and his discouragement was only temporary, but he retained his anonymity and took the precaution of signing himself "M. Eugène" for a while.

Like most early nineteenth-century playwrights, he worked in collaboration; he and Germain Delavigne wrote their early *comédies-vaudevilles* together. The form was simple and in the tradition of the eighteenth-century pastoral: a single act in stylized (some said stilted) prose, interspersed with songs in rhymed couplets. He learned and imitated the form carefully, but the next few years saw a series of resounding failures. *Les Dervis*, at the Vaudeville (September 2, 1811), written with Delavigne, was pitilessly massacred by the public; *L'Auberge, ou les Brigands sans le savoir*, with Charles Délestre-Poirson, was somewhat better received, but could by no means be counted an overwhelming success. An attempt at *opéra-comique, La Chambre à coucher*, and *Koulikan*, a three-act melodrama, both written in collaboration with the banker Jean-Henri Dupin, had similar receptions, as did

Thibault, Comte de Champagne, again with Delavigne. In front of the sophisticated and uninhibited Parisian audience he was learning a difficult craft in its most exacting form, the one-act play. His reception seemed to be warming, but any real optimism about his future must have been tempered by three successive failures in 1814 and 1815: *Thomas le chanceux, ou les trois bossus, Barbanéra, ou la Nuit des noces* and *Le Bachelier de Salamanque*. Two more *opéras-comiques, La Perruque et la redingote* and *La Comtesse de Troun*, were added to the heap of failures, and one is tempted to speculate that Scribe himself might have begun to doubt his choice of profession.

At this time, political events may have distracted his audience from such light entertainment. Napoleon's calamitous Russian campaign, followed by his abdication in April 1814, put the country into a state of chaos. Scribe, however, was far more attuned to theatrical affairs than to governmental change. On May 20, 1815, in the midst of the Hundred Days, he and Dupin brought *La Mort et le Bûcheron* to the Vaudeville, and for the first time gained some approval; in October, they repeated the experience with *Le Gascon, La Pompe funèbre*.

He was accepted, but having yet to achieve real success, he persevered with determination. Delavigne, on the other hand, was becoming discouraged; none of the three plays they had written together had been well received, and he lacked Scribe's energetic optimism. Their aims and ambitions also differed sharply; Delavigne wrote better couplets than Scribe, but his theatrical imagination was considerably weaker. He retired from the stage and, with his brother Casimir, devoted himself to poetry. The parting was amicable and they remained close friends; both Delavignes eventually wrote operas, but they never failed to consult their former schoolmate on the intricacies of plot structure, nor did Scribe hesitate to request their assistance on lyrics.

III   *Dramatic Success*

Meanwhile he wrote with others. A collaborative effort with Délestre-Poirson brought him his first genuine success. When on November 4, 1815, *Une nuit de la Garde nationale* opened at the Vaudeville to thunderous applause, his seven years of apprenticeship were at last over. Accidentally or deliberately, this *comédie-vaudeville* was an innovation, both in his own work and on the boulevard stage. Scribe had applied his well-developed theatrical technique in a manner that was quite distinct from the fanciful pastorals: the subject was contemporary, the treatment realistic and the language colloquial. The National Guard was greatly respected by Parisians for their services in recent months when the city had been twice occupied by foreign troops. Respect, however, did not prevent even members of the Guard from laughing at the gentle satire. He had found the formula for success, although he himself did not yet realize it. His next three efforts failed as dismally as his earlier attempts; not until February of 1816, again with Délestre-Poirson, did he sound the right note with *Flore et Zéphire*.

Scribe was at ease with the tradition of collaboration; when he was older and had reached the pinnacle of his career, he explained that "the few works I wrote alone were for me hard work, those I wrote with my collaborators, a pleasure."[7] That the pleasure was genuine is evident in his generosity to his co-authors, invariably sharing with them not only the revenue but the glory. His collaborators remained his life-long friends, and his history is not marred with incidents of ill-feeling. He was grateful for their ideas and, while he always did the major share of the work, he gave them credit in the bills, a share of the profits and dedicated the first complete edition of his plays to them.

Collaboration, along with his work habits, may account for the extraordinary fecundity of his pen. The total number of his plays may never be known; almost four hundred have been documented, but his frequent use of pseudonyms has prevented an accurate accounting. Although by the time of *Une nuit de la Garde nationale* he was no longer a vulnerable fledgling in need of protection, he sometimes still chose to conceal his name, listing himself as "Deschamps," "Nicomède," "Félix" or "Etienne," perhaps because his own name appeared so often on the playbills. Between 1815 and 1820, he was responsible for at least sixty-five plays. Most were one-act *comédies-vaudevilles*, but the list also included longer plays, comic operas and even some three-act melodramas.

On the surface, his career progressed smoothly, yet it was not an unbroken line of success, and there were times when he was the target of jealous animosity. In 1817, after the celebrated *Le Solliciteur* (which Schlegel preferred to *Le Misanthrope*), he and Dupin wrote *Le Combat des montagnes*, presented at the Variétés on July 12. It was a topical little comedy, but the reverberations it produced were heard all over the city.

The circumstances seemed fashioned for the subject. Toward the end of 1816, a new amusement appeared in Paris—"*montagnes*," a primitive form of the roller coaster built on a wooden frame. The idea, imported from Russia, was instantly and enthusiastically adopted, and within a few months the "*montagnes russes*" had been supplemented by Swiss, Illyrian and Egyptian "mountains." In the public gardens of the city and provinces and on the estates of the wealthy, the machines ran all day long and, lighted by gas, far into the night. They were exciting and dangerous—the king of Prussia had broken his nose on one—and they were the subject of much discussion before the vogue ceased.

The "mountains" were amusing and an ideal topic for Scribe's gentle comedy, except for one brief scene that provoked the storm. The incident seemed innocent enough. It happened that at the moment, it was the fashion among young store clerks, to assume the moustache, black cravat and scarlet *boutonnière* of the military, and when Brunet, playing Calicot, a "merchant of novelties," was jokingly mistaken for a soldier, every clerk in the audience felt a personal affront. On the third night, a great furor in the house nearly ended the performance, and a number of clerks announced they would barricade the theater. Soldiers were posted as the threats grew louder, and a barrage of pamphlets, caricatures and newspaper stories appeared in the "Calicot War."[8]

Actually, the uproar enhanced the box office sales, but Scribe and Dupin, astonished at the fury, set about at once to calm the outraged clerks. In two days they had put together *Le Café des Variétés*, a public apology that turned their satire toward the theater. It opened August, 5, three weeks after the battle began and produced exactly the right effect. The clerks were properly pacified, and everyone was charmed.

IV   *Popular Acclaim*

The following year, two more topical comedies were unreservedly applauded. *Une Visite à Bedlam*, with Délestre-Poirson, dealt with the military occupation of several frontier departments; *l'Hôtel des Quatre Nations*, with Dupin and a former clerk now a well-known playwright, Nicholas Brazier, celebrated their liberation. By 1820, Scribe was the most popular playwright in Paris, and his imprint was firmly fixed on the Parisian theater. The pastoral style had disappeared, replaced by clever, amusing plays set in contemporary time and depending on current events for their subjects. Young authors regarded him as a genius and eagerly sought his advice; women looked upon the eligible young bachelor as fair prey and vied for his attention.

In 1820, his friends and sometime collaborators, Charles Délestre-Poirson and Alphonse Cerfbeer, made an agreement with La Roserie to establish the Gymnase on the Rue de Chartres. On December 23, the theater opened with *Le Boulevard Bonne-Nouvelle* by Scribe and two friends who had also abandoned law for the stage, Joseph Duveyrier, who called himself Mélesville, and Charles Moreau. It was the beginning of a long association. Délestre-Poirson promptly signed Scribe to a contract that obliged the writer to produce only for the Gymnase. The agreement was not absolute, for Scribe continued to supply both the Variétés and the Vaudeville with new works and, later, the Opéra-Comique and the Comédie-Française as well.

Délestre-Poirson was an excellent manager; within a few months, he assumed the sole management of the Gymnase, and in 1824, the Duchess de Berry became its patron. In her honor, the Gymnase then became the Théâtre de Madame and, by being frequented by the court, the most socially acceptable of the boulevard theaters.

The incredible flow of work continued. In the decade between 1820 and 1830, Scribe gave the Gymnase one-hundred-five plays, in addition to those written for other theaters: the Opéra-Comique (eighteen), the Opéra (six), the Vaudeville (four), the Variétés (five) and three long works for the Comédie-Française. Besides these were the occasional works: one each for the Théâtre de la Pigalle, the Théâtre des Nouveautés and the Théâtre de Bruxelles, two for the Gaîté and two for the Odéon. In all, an astonishing total of 149 plays.

V *Scribe's Technique*

Such a prolific pen does not always maintain a high standard—and some of his works would have benefited from revision. As a whole, however, the opus is surprisingly good and, while some of the credit may go to his collaborators, most of it belongs to Scribe alone. He was extraordinarily sensitive to the demands of the performance and what makes a play "work" on the stage: the dynamics of plot, the tensions that build to a climax, the rhythm of speech suitable for actors, and a hundred other details that seem insignificant on the page but give a play vital energy when it is before an audience.

The secret is in the situations Scribe builds for his characters. He had a true genius for plot structure and for keeping the attention of the audience focused in one direction while he skilfully prepared a surprising yet perfectly logical *dénouement*. Over and over the impossible becomes the possible, near-tragedy is transformed into hilarious comedy, and the complicated knot untied in a wholly unforeseen manner. The formula worked for nineteenth-century French audiences as it works today. Yet even Scribe was not infallible. Sometimes seemingly sure successes proved to be failures. In those cases, it was reported, he smiled, rubbed his hands and exclaimed, "I'll do it over next year!"[9] With his amazing facility, he could do just that.

He has been charged with a lack of originality, and perhaps rightfully so. Yet this fault, if it indeed is one, derived from a combination of his talent, his social situation and his personality. He could see and develop dramatic possibilities in any idea. Friends, strangers and would-be playwrights of all kinds bombarded him with poorly written pieces, suggestions and pleas for help. They were rarely disappointed by an author whose kindness was as legendary as his facility with the pen.

Once, in 1821, Dupin brought him a two-act vaudeville needing extensive repairs. Scribe, as he usually did, promised to look it over and see what could be done. A few weeks later, he invited Dupin to dinner and the theater for the opening of a sparkling new one-act, *Michel et Christine*. Dupin not only failed to recognize his own idea in the play he enjoyed immensely, but did not, until it was over and an actor stepped forth to announce "Scribe and Dupin" as its authors, realize what his friend had done.

Scribe teased him, "It's a bad father who doesn't recognize his own children!"

"Parbleu," Dupin replied, "Who could when they are changed at nurse?"[10]

A year later, the librettist, Jules-Henri de Saint-Georges, brought him an idea that turned on a game of lansquenet, a card game that had been popular in the eighteenth century.

"You are wasting your time," Scribe told him, "If you want to use a card game on the stage, it must be familiar to your audience today—*écarté*, for example." When he had finished showing how it could be done, Saint-Georges remarked that now it needed only to be written down. Scribe smiled, and on November 14, 1822, *Ecarté*, "by MM. Scribe, Mélesville and Saint-Georges" was successfully produced at the Gymnase.[11]

Such facility brought considerable reward. Scribe could have lived comfortably, if modestly, on his inheritance, but he was no amateur writing for pleasure alone. Neither was he greedy, however; he simply asked and received a fair price for his work. Early in his career, he had been glad to get a hundred francs, payable in books, for the printing rights to *L'Auberge*, but by 1822, the publisher of *Valérie* was happy to offer him three thousand francs[12]—in addition to the profits from the theater.

VI   *Entry into the Comédie-Française*

Valérie was the first of his plays to be performed at the Comédie-Française, and the events leading up to it were unusual. Originally written with Mélesville for Léontine Fay, one of the Gymnase stars, it was quickly revised when she fell ill before rehearsals began. Scribe restructured the plot into three acts, cut out the couplets and changed one line of dialogue for the Comédie. There the leading role of the blind heroine was given to Mademoiselle Mars, whose brilliant portrayal added much to the lustre of the play and assured its favorable reception.

Scribe's unbroken stream of work, the high prices he commanded and his ever increasing popularity with the public naturally produced some jealousy. For the most part, his attackers were those who had never worked with him. Though he himself never answered their charges, his friends defended him strongly. At a banquet, Pierre-Frédéric Carmouche once silenced an obstreperous young vaudevillist loudly proclaiming that Scribe's success was due to his collaborators, "If one figures the proportions, it will be seen that Monsieur Scribe's contribution is only one in forty."

Carmouche, noting that the young man had never even met Scribe, said dryly, "I can prove you are wrong."

"And how can you do that?"

"By personal experience. I have written between twelve and fifteen plays with him, and I swear to you that in all of them, there is not one word of mine."[13]

By the late twenties, he was a millionaire with an income of sixty-thousand francs a year, a mansion on the fashionable Rue Olivier-Saint-Georges and a country house at Montalais, where a sign on the gate of "Séricourt" greeted visitors with a frank:

> The theatre paid for this lovely place too;
> Thanks, passer-by—perhaps I owe you.[14]

He lived well and was careful with his money, but he was by no means avaricious. When his former college needed repairs, Scribe, now one of the principal adminstrators, subscribed seventy-thousand francs.

He never spoke of his private benefactions, but one of his close friends, Xavier Saintine, discovered one quite by accident. Saintine, anxious to complete a play they were writing, called at Scribe's house one day and found his way barred by a mass of people in the street, under the *porte-cochère* and up the stairs to the door. Curious, he asked who they were and why they were there. He was informed that they were neighborhood workers temporarily out of work because of a local recession. Scribe was providing each family with a monthly sum to live on until the labor situation improved. This had gone on for months and continued for several more, but Saintine, an intimate of the house, had never heard a word of it until he happened to meet the workers.[15] This was only one instance of Scribe's generosity; in all, he spent more than five-hundred-thousand francs on similar philanthropies, dowries and gifts.

Another aspect of his generosity took the form of time, as when a Madame Friedelle, a former schoolmistress, "of a certain age," asked for advice on a play. He protested, quite honestly, that he was too busy to read it, but she insisted on leaving it with him. The next day he learned the lady was destitute, and, dropping his own play, revised her play, took it to Délestre-Poirson and insisted it be done at the Gymnase—all within six weeks. It opened to a modest success on June 11, 1825, and Madame Friedelle reaped a small and much needed profit. Her collaborator, listed as "Alexandre," did not claim his share.

The good Samaritan came to regret his act; a few days later, Madame Friedelle arrived at his door bearing two more manuscripts. It was clearly to be a long association, and only a master plotter could have devised his escape with a solution satisfactory to all. He called his agent, Guyot, and ordered that twelve hundred francs be paid out annually for the authors' rights, one half supposedly to "Alexandre," and the other to Madame Friedelle, thus ensuring she would have six hundred francs a year, at that time an adequate income. After this, the lady visited Scribe almost daily, with new stories, until he was forced to escape to the country. She never knew the true story of her good fortune; although she collected her "royalties" for the rest of her life, she was always a trifle scandalized to see Scribe write forty or fifty plays with Mélesville while, she said, "he had worked only once with her."[16]

VII   *The July Revolution*

It is generally assumed that the July Revolution of 1830 marked a turning point in Scribe's mode of writing, that from that point, his plays became heavier in subject and tone. To some extent this is true; most of his more serious plays were written in the last half of his career, although he never lost his essential lightness of heart. Yet his basic moral view was always serious, and at least two works of the 1820s have as a foundation social issue.

Le Mariage de raison (1822), a *comédie-vaudeville* written with François-Antoine Varner, was the first to deal directly with the money question in relation to marriage. Two years later, *Le Mariage d'argent* (1824), explored the question further. Both were timely; Romanticism was in full bloom, and, although Scribe did not join in the Classic/Romantic war, his roots were in the eighteenth century, and he defended the concept of a reasonable life, over against the advocates of free passion. "Reason" in his terms meant honoring the authority of parents and the sanctity of the marriage vows. Happy (i.e. reasonable) marriages required consonant personalities, mutual esteem, equality of social rank and a sound financial basis. Romantic love was unstable at best, chimerical at worst, and a sure road to tragedy.

Scribe's theatrical talent prevented his message from becoming tiresomely didactic. His satire aimed equally at the exaggerated romantic imagination and at the stolid pragmatism that allowed for no dreams at all. His gifts included the ability to charm an audience whose members ranged from the Chaussée-d'Antin to the Faubourg Saint-Germain, whom he was able to make laugh at themselves without anger. Nevertheless, social and moral standards are evident in both plays, and when the audience so chose, the lesson could be learned.

Social consciousness is not as obvious in his works as in his life

He was not only generous to his collaborators (chosen or otherwise), but to unknown writers as well. A man who had achieved so much both in reputation and financial security might well have become smug. He could easily have looked upon the less fortunate as did the majority of his class, who regarded poverty as the result of character flaws. Perhaps because he had worked with many whose poverty was circumstantial rather than arisen from inherent weakness, or perhaps because he was part of a system in which managers commonly took outrageous advantage of struggling writers, he was aware of injustice. In 1827, he moved to do something about it and, with a number of other authors, established the Société des Auteurs et Compositeurs Dramatiques.

The idea was not entirely new. In 1780, Beaumarchais had formed an association of playwrights to standardize fees and work for a law, finally passed in 1791, forbidding the presentation of plays without the author's permission; but the earlier agreement was never enforced, and the law did not touch on the question of payment. In 1807, another society of writers published a list of standard fees for provincial theaters; in Paris, only the Vaudeville observed it. In all other theaters, managers and authors made arrangements for each play, usually to the disadvantage of the latter. Scribe commanded the highest prices, but he was acutely unhappy about the situation, as he later said:

When I wrote my first vaudeville, in 1811, authors had absolute freedom, nothing was forbidden them; nothing restricted them, but also nothing safeguarded their works to any manager; on the other hand, the managers could buy according to their pleasure! Their pleasure was to pay as little as possible, and they had an embarrassment of riches—plays were then commissioned at a discount! One of the deans of that era, one whose talents and success should have assured him the most favorable conditions, was Désaugiers . . . Désaugiers had seen one of his works, La Chatte merveilleuse, play five hundred successive times at the Variétés, at 4,000 francs per performance. That is to say, during nearly two years, the work never left the boards a single night and brought almost two million francs to the management. Well, this cat—or rather this goose that laid golden eggs—produced for its authors, Messieurs Désaugiers and Gentil, only one louis each performance, bringing them no more than two hundred fifty louis apiece![17]

The new Société des Auteurs et Compositeurs Dramatiques had

four stated aims: to prevent managers from uniting against an author and "freezing" him out; to establish fair rights for authors in Parisian as well as provincial theaters; to establish a fund for needy authors and their heirs; to establish a common fund for operating and other expenses. One franc and twenty centimes would be assessed from each play presented by the members for this purpose. Theaters not observing the Société's rules were not permitted to produce members' plays, and members who allowed their works to be played in such theaters would be fined.

It was an equitable arrangement and ensured just treatment by both sides; new playwrights would have at least a fair minimum, successful ones could demand what the traffic would bear. Scribe served on the seventeen-member commission, although he was not elected president until the last two years of his life.

When the July Revolution removed the Bourbons from power and replaced them with the July Monarchy of Louis-Philippe, the association of the Théâtre de Madame with the Duchess de Berry, now in exile, became a distinct disadvantage. The theater closed during the disturbances and reopened in August as the Gymnase again, but even with two new plays by Scribe, [18] audiences remained cool and the house was seldom filled.

The seemingly impossible had happened. Not only the theater, but Scribe himself fell out of favor. When his next work for the Gymnase, *La Protectrice et le ministre*, appeared in November, there was little applause, and the plays which followed fared no better. He turned to opera, a form not completely new to him, for he had dozens of *opéras-comiques* and ballets to his credit and had written two full-length operas as early as 1828. His libretti were excellent, for he had a fine musical ear and an understanding of singers' problems.

VIII   *The Opera*

When *Le Philtre* appeared in June, 1831, a two-act work with music by Auber, almost at once Scribe began also to write *Robert le Diable* for Meyerbeer. Twenty-two more operas were to follow, with a list of composers that included the names of Adam, Bellini, Cherubini, Gounod, Halévy, Rossini, Thomas and Verdi.

Working with Meyerbeer was demanding; the composer was seldom certain what he wanted. He once rejected a completed three-act libretto because he wanted a fourth act septet to unite the characters. Scribe tried to explain that adding a full act was not a simple piece of patchwork but required a restructuring of the entire piece. No matter, Meyerbeer wanted his septet. When Scribe had obliged him, he changed his mind again and decided a simple monologue would suffice.[19]

On another occasion, he asked Scribe for "eight-syllable verses in regular form," but when he saw them, he announced, "The regular form is absurd," and demanded ten-syllable verses. After a dozen revisions, he decided he didn't like the subject; but when Scribe reminded him that it had been chosen by the composer, not the librettist, Meyerbeer remarked calmly, "We were both mistaken."[20]

Robert le Diable presented only one real obstacle, a special poem for a special air. Scribe asked Casimir, then Germain Delavigne, to write some lines, but neither could please the composer. Time grew short, Meyerbeer wanted to leave for the country, and nothing had been found acceptable. At last, just as Meyerbeer was getting into his carriage, Scribe quickly scribbled five lines on a scrap of paper and gave them to him:

> Robert, o my true love,
> I put my trust in thee.
> My frightened soul you see:
> Grace to you from above,
>
> And grace as well for me.

Meyerbeer read them and smiled, "I have my air."[21]

IX   *The 1830s*

Other critics being less than pleased, it was during the 1830s that Scribe suffered the first serious attacks on his work. Gustave Planche regarded *Dix Ans de la vie d'une femme* (1832) as immoral and debauched, a view that must have shocked Scribe's conservative soul. He was defended by Sainte-Beuve, however, who told of a young girl planning to elope with an unsuitable young man but who, after seeing the play, gave up her plans and confessed all to her mother.[22] Such direct results are rare, but this one served to refute Planche and must have also eased Scribe's mind. There is no doubt that the solid bourgeois values of honesty, filial obedience and morality were important to him. He lived by them, and he embodied them in every play he wrote; even his lightest comedies hold them sacred.

The plays of this decade and after usually have a perceptibly serious base and turn on a moral point, sometimes with a political or historical background. It is tempting to ascribe the change to personal causes: his age, his declining favor, the change in government that placed him outside the circles of power. Such elements may have played a part in altering his point of view, but it is more likely to have been a result of Scribe's sensitivity to a change in the taste of his audience.

Whatever the cause, the pattern is clear in *Bertrand et Raton*, a "serious" five-act comedy he wrote for the Comédie-Française. Based on the fall of the minister Struensée,[23] the play contains one of Scribe's most memorable characters, Bertrand de Ranzau, and is based on a favorite theme: great effects result from small causes. It was well received, although some critics objected to the premise, insisting that great political changes could result only from great minds and actions. History has validated Scribe's point, and the play remains a classic of its kind.

A month later, *Une chanoinesse* was given at the Gymnase, a one-act melodrama, one of several Francis Cornu had optimistically brought up from the country and asked Scribe to read. When he returned for advice three months later, Scribe asked if he had time to listen to a new play and Cornu, flattered, acquiesced. Like so many others, he was surprised to find himself a collaborator on an excellent vaudeville. Scribe explained, "I found an idea in your melodrama—for me one idea is enough."[24] It played the first of many performances at the Gymnase on the last day of the year.

1834 saw a slight abatement of the flood that had deluged Paris for over twenty years. Only nine Scribe works were given a première, four at the Gymnase, three at the Opéra-Comique and two at the Comédie-Française. The fact that the latter were full-length and written without collaboration may explain the diminution in number. One of these is particularly worth remarking, *L'Ambitieux*, another long, serious comedy set in the eighteenth century at the time of Robert Walpole's fall. Again his theme deals with a small cause—two minor love affairs—and the result, an historic change of government. The play's satiric references to the July Revolution were not lost on his audience, and the reception was mixed. On the whole, it was favorable, however, and *Figaro* pointed out the unusual appeal in "the character of the ambitious man from a special point of view—not the climber who wishes to rise, but one who cannot decide to descend, and who, having once come down, again aspires to rise."[25]

X   Scribe in the Académie

These plays, weightier in theme if not tone, combined with the sheer volume of work that had preceded them, may have led to the honor that was about to be bestowed on him, a seat in the renowned Académie Française where, so many years before, he had received the laurel wreath from Arnault. Ironically, it was Arnault he was replacing. The old playwright had died in 1834, and, after some debate, Scribe was elected to fill the chair that had once been occupied by Racine. Not all his colleagues were overjoyed; at least one, remarking sourly on Scribe's collaborators, was heard to comment, "We shouldn't give him a chair but a bench!"[26]

Théodore-Ferdinand Vallon de Villeneuve provided an answer in his welcoming speech; to Scribe he said, "Without them you might not have written so much, but without you they would not have succeeded at all."[27]

On January 28, 1836, Villeneuve officially presented Scribe to the august assemblage, and the playwright gave his opening address. It was a modest and traditional speech which began by recalling his initiation to the domed Institute where he had first seen Arnault. He presented a eulogy of his predecessor with a brief biography and review of his plays, as well as a tribute to Arnault's talents for writing lyrics. From this he led into an astonishing thesis that seemed to disclaim any importance for his own work: it is not the theater that reflects a nation, but its songs.

Someone had once claimed, he said, that if all books except dramatic comedies were burned, the nation's history could be reconstructed through them alone. Scribe denied this, "I do not think the comic author should be an historian," said the master of comedy, "that is not his mission; I do not believe that in Molière himself can one recover the history of our country."[28] The comic writer works in reverse, he explained, because people go to the theater to be taken out of their daily lives. During the decadent Regency (1715 - 1723), comedy was in the "cold, correct, pretentious but decent" plays of Destouches, the pathos of La Chaussée; under Louis XV, "or rather, under Voltaire" the intellectual, fantasy and empty romance flourished. The horrors of the Revolution produced scenes of "humanity and charity, of sentiment," while the Restoration, not Napoleon's Empire, saw the glorification of arms. On the other hand, the song maker, an "auxiliary of history" spoke of contemporary names and dates, of specific events; when the theater was strictly regulated, song became the sole expression of the people. Songmakers had fought for the nation's freedom and, he concluded rather sadly, now that it had been achieved, the song was dead, having no further purpose:

While, in our time, the tomb of monarchy has also been that of the song, let us hope, for the good of the country, that it will never be reborn, that our liberty will be defended by others, and that the eulogy I have just spoken may be its funeral oration.[29]

It was a graceful tribute to Arnault's talent and a patriotic declaration, given in a spirit of humble gratitude; but it was poorly received by the press who ridiculed Scribe as a pretentious songster claiming unwarranted glory for himself.

Scribe, with the Parisian stage to air his views, did not respond in kind—unless the satire of *La Camaraderie* (1837) can be interpreted as an answer. In it, he pokes fun at the backbiting and puerile intrigues of mediocre bureaucrats. He had treated the subject earlier in *Le Solliciteur*, but that had been a one-act vaudeville; this was a five-act drama for the Comédie-Française in which he had ample opportunity to riposte. Yet nowhere is there an indication that his satire has a personal target; rather, it is directed against an evil any Frenchman of the day could recognize: the triumph of mediocrity within the governmental establishment resulting from the exchange of favors among the ruling clique.

Not everything was grim during these years, for he was a vital part of the artistic world. His work at the various theaters brought him into contact not only with his fellow-playwrights but with composers, painters and performers of all kinds. Among the latter, he was friendly with many dancers and had written for them as early as 1827 when he had given the highly esteemed choreographer, Aumer, credit as co-author of *La Somnambule*. Aumer died in 1832, and six years later Scribe found a new collaborator in the great ballerina Fanny Ellsler; for her he created the title role in *La Volière*.[30]

XI *Marriage*

For all his rich professional and social life, Scribe may have begun to feel lonely. At the age of forty-eight he married. Rumor had it he was trying to escape the marriage-minded ladies who still pursued him, though this may be doubted. Characteristically, he did not rush into his new state; his bride was a woman he had known for several years. He had met her first at the home of the poet, Béranger, where she had come to borrow a book. He asked about her and was informed she was the wife of Béranger's friend, M. Biollay, a wine merchant. Scribe said no more, but after her husband's death, he began to visit her, and when a suitable time had intervened, they were married.

It was a happy union; they had much in common both in artistic tastes and in social awareness; in the country, where they spent much of their time, Madame Scribe was known for her kindness and good works. She had two sons from her former marriage, but the step-relationship was quite the opposite of fairy tale tradition. Scribe was a loving father, and the boys returned the sentiment. The only hint of disagreement between husband and wife is in an anecdote about their life at Séricourt. Madame Scribe, worried about her husband's insatiable appetite for work, tried to interest him in one of her passions, gardening. The sophisticated Parisian was not fascinated with planting, weeding and pruning, but after a time he seemed less reluctant, and indeed appeared to be absorbed by one section of the shrubbery. When Madame Scribe sought him out to congratulate him on his new avocation, she found him seated on an overturned flowerpot, finishing a new play.[31] She may have been correct in her insistence that her husband need not drive himself so furiously, but she could not wean him completely from the habits of a lifetime. She must have had some influence, however, for the total number of plays written in the twenty-two years of his marriage is less than that of any previous decade.

Many of the later works are longer and display his remarkable ability in dramatic construction. In moving away from the eighteenth century, he did much more than merely change the tone from elegant fantasy to realism, he also altered the approach to structure itself. Carefully prepared exposition in the first act gave the audience all the necessary information for the complex development in which not a line is wasted, no extraneous characters appear, and all threads are tied off in the end. In short, he created the "well-made" play that would be exploited more fully by the next generation of French playwrights. His most prominent follower and successor to the crown of popularity, Victorien Sardou, advised all young aspirants to "Read Scribe! Read Scribe! You will learn theatre from him!"[32] The later plays are often concerned with social questions, and although he is neither an historian nor a reformer, he foreshadows the sober thesis plays of Ibsen. The great Norwegian followed Sardou's advice to the letter, and his plays clearly show Scribe's influence. If Ibsen is to be considered the "Father of Modern Drama," Scribe must undoubtedly be regarded as its grandfather.

Although he never lost his fundamentally comic view—in the end everything must work out happily—*La Calomnie* and *Une chaîne* are examples of more thoughtful work. The first shows the devastating effects of malicious gossip on a small town, the second, the difficulties of escaping from illicit romantic entanglements. *Le Verre d'eau* came between *La Calomnie* and *Une chaîne;* like *Bertrand et Raton* and *L'Ambitieux*, it exemplifies his thesis of great events and small causes. In this case, a spilled glass of water brings about the fall of Marlborough and the Whig regime. The similarity to the earlier plays goes further than theme; like them it is set in the eighteenth century and, like a dozen more, deals with English history. It is not clear how well Scribe knew the language, but he did visit England, and he is listed as the cotranslator of *L'Irlandais* (1831); also, at least two of his operas, *La Tempête* (1850) and *Florinda* (1851) had their premiere performances in London.

Nor had he lost his light touch. In *Oscar, ou le Mari qui trompe sa femme* (1842), he spins a frothy tale of a man who tries unsuccessfully to deceive his wife. The play stayed in the repertory for almost forty years and is still a fine playable script, but, like so many of his comedies, does not appear advantageously in the library and has received little critical attention from scholars. Francisque Sarcey, however, applauded the ease with which Scribe moved events too rapidly to permit analysis—the essence of good structure. The theater experience, as Sarcey phrased it, was "a contract between author and auditor," and he used *Oscar* as an example: the play was "improbable, absurd, monstrous and ignoble"—and a superb theatrical experience.[33]

Meanwhile, Scribe not only experimented in modes of drama but in other genres as well. All his life he had written verse for his plays and operas, now he also began to write short stories, novels and proverbs. Works like *Carlo Broschi*, the "memoirs of a gentleman," the romantic *Filleul d'Amadis, ou les Amours d'une fée* and *Fleurette*, the story of a flower girl, brought him much profit but added nothing to his reputation. It was said that *Le Siècle* paid him sixty thousand francs for the serial rights to *Piquillo Alliagra*,[34] a long and rather dreary history of the Moors under Philip III, scarcely read at the time and not at all since.

He had achieved early and consistent popularity, but now after thirty years, a new generation with new ideas appeared. Younger writers like Alexandre Dumas fils and Théophile Gautier challenged his place on Olympus. Ignoring his very real contribution to the theater, they regarded him as hopelessly old-fashioned and out of touch with "reality." Dumas fils, as steeped in Scribe's craftsmanship as in his own father's romanticism, was particularly virulent, and Gautier, with his critic's pen, wielded an even more lasting force.

XII   *Changing Tastes*

The careful, slow exposition bored the younger generation, while the complicated plots seemed artificial and useless to men concerned with social problems and ideals. Scribe was trivial, they said, an antiquated carpenter who built situations not characters, whose colloquial language was unworthy of an artist, and who had nothing to offer the modern audience. They could not deny his continuing appeal to audiences, but they dismissed it as the verdict of a populace notoriously incapable of appreciating true art.

In part they were right; Scribe had continued to write in the manner he pioneered, but what they did not (or chose not to) understand was that the manner was based on the essential demands of the medium. It worked because it observed the needs of the performance, and even as they attacked him, they followed his precepts in constructing their own plays.

It is possible that had Scribe remained as intimate with the theater as in earlier years, he might have altered his own mode to keep pace with the new. There is no reason to suppose he could not change, and he was no mere hack repeating a formula, but he had moved out of the theatrical vanguard. Not only was he experimenting with nondramatic forms, but his personal life absorbed much of his attention. One of his stepsons married the daughter of an old friend, Jean-François-Alfred Bayard, whom Scribe had found an execrable collaborator but now welcomed as a member of the family. Such events drew his attention away from what had been the center of his world for most of his life. Yet not being ready to retire from the scene, he regularly provided new productions for both the Opéra and the Opéra-Comique.

The number of his works had become enormous, and one story has it that when a collection was to be published, he tried to prepare an alphabetical list of titles. He discovered that three letters were not represented: K, X and Y, whereupon he immediately wrote *Le Kiosque* for the Opéra-Comique, *Xacarilla* for the Opéra and *Yelva* for the Gymnase.[35] It is a pretty story, no doubt designed to display his skill, but it is, unfortunately, not true. The theaters and plays are correct, but *Yelva* appeared in 1828, *Xacarilla* in 1839 and *Le Kiosque* in 1842. Moreover, "K" had been done in the 1813 melodrama, *Koulikan*. At no time during these widely spaced years could he have sat down and dashed off the three plays.

Despite the increasingly frequent attacks, Scribe had neither ceased to be popular nor himself become defensive; his appraisal of his own work was still modest. In 1849, when the Théâtre de la République asked him to write a comedy for the great star, Rachel, he was doubtful about his own ability and asked Emile Legouvé to collaborate. It was not a diplomatic choice. The previous year, Legouvé had offered Rachel his *Médée* (later a favorite of Ristori), and she had refused it. Scribe admired Legouvé, however, and requested him to find a suitable subject. Legouvé agreed and chose an incident well suited to Scribe's own thesis of cause and effect, the anecdote of Lecouvreur's throwing the lines:

> I am not one of those hardy women
> Who, feeling at peace in the midst of crime,
> Knows how to remain serene and never blush!

into the face of the Duchess de Bouillon, sitting in the stage box.[36]

The play had everything to appeal to the actress: dramatic entrances and exits, scenes of high emotion and a character already sympathetic to a French audience.[37] When it was finished, Scribe threw his arms around Legouvé and exclaimed, "A hundred performances at 6,000 francs!" Rachel, however, refused it until lengthy and intense persuasion by the theater managers convinced her to try it. Only then did she learn what Scribe had realized at the moment of completion, and *Adrienne Lecouvreur* became a triumph not only for Rachel but for Bernhardt and Modjeska later.

Rachel, who changed her opinion of the two playwrights, was pleased to accept their next offering, *Bataille de dames* (1851), considered Scribe's best play by English critics, perhaps because for many years it was the only one translated into their language. Brander Matthews called it a masterpiece, remarking, "The comedy of intrigue can go no further: this is its last word."[38] In the eyes of audiences, it merited more than the hundred performances of *Adrienne Lecouvreur* and continued a popular favorite well into the twentieth century.

Audiences and actors continued to favor Scribe; young poets did not, and they had their allies in certain newspapers. On January 26, 1855, Gérard de Nerval was found hanged, a victim of poverty, despair and madness. There was no doubt that it was suicide, but four years later, Philippe Audébrand began a series of attacks, using the suicide as one of his main charges. His paper, *La Gazette de Paris*, and another, *Le Charivari*, published articles calling Scribe's election to the Académie Française an insult to that body and impugning the playwright's honesty by saying he refused to pay for work he had ordered. The third charge was more emotional: Audébrand claimed that Scribe had flooded the theatrical market with worthless plays and, by preventing Gérard de Nerval from a fair hearing, had pushed him to his death. As proof, he printed a letter from Nerval to Monrose, director of the Théâtre Royal at the Hague on the occasion of an 1852 command performance. Nerval had asked that one of his plays be presented, but Monrose had wisely chosen Scribe's *Le Vieux Château*, and the theater had profited from it. Monrose had explained to Nerval as gently as possible that among so many good French poets, one must choose the most outstanding ["qui tient la corde"]; Nerval answered, "And that cord strangles you." Audébrand postdated the letter and changed "you" to "us," giving a sinister and prophetic cast to Nerval's words when he published it.

Of the three charges, the first did not touch Scribe at all; it was already hackneyed. The second was easily refuted as an attempt to throw a bad light on an unimportant business transaction: Scribe had hired a young artist named Héreau to paint some panels for his new house on the Rue Pigalle, but when the work was finished, Scribe felt it was shoddy and would pay only for the materials. Héreau had not objected legally, but he had bruited the story about Paris, and Audébrand's use of it discredited Scribe's honor. The third charge, with its "proofs," was especially ugly, for its very nature was sensational and polarized opinion on both sides.

Scribe, usually the gentlest of men, reacted with implacable severity against injustice and calumny; against the advice of his friend Etienne de Biéville, editor of *Le Siècle*, he sued both papers for libel. He won a clear victory. On January 21, 1859, *Le Charivari* was ordered to pay court costs and to publish the judgment of the court in its pages, with a fine of fifty francs for each day's delay. On February 11, *La Gazette de Paris* was given stiffer penalties: both Audébrand and the publisher, Dallingen, were sentenced to three months in prison and fined two thousand francs each. They were also ordered to pay the court costs and to print a notice of the judgment in three papers of Scribe's choice. With such a verdict, Scribe was entitled to press for damages, but he did not; the miscreants had suffered enough. Audébrand was publicly disgraced, and Dallingen was ruined; on March 17, he sold his paper to *Le Figaro*.[39]

The ending was worthy of Monte Cristo, but Scribe took no glory in it. He continued to work as always, concentrating more and more on musical dramas that did not demand social messages. The "flood" dwindled to a trickle, but almost all of the new works were full-length and, in the case of the opreas, have maintained a lasting appeal—works such as *Le Prophète*, *La Dame de Pique*, *Les Vêpres Siciliennes* and *L'Africaine*.

XIII *End of a Career*

Nearly seventy now, he showed no signs of weakness, his work as energetic as ever, the ideas embodied with consummate skill. He had been actively involved in French theater for over fifty years, and had contributed much to its prestige throughout Europe and to that of playwrights within the country. In the provinces, his name was used indiscriminately to indicate a good play: *Tartuffe*, *Lucrèce*, *Andromaque* and *Le Cid* were all listed as "by M. Scribe." His motto pointed to the reason: a pen crossed over Pan-pipes above the words, "Inde Fortuna et Libertas."

The end came on February 20, 1861. He had been at a meeting with Auguste Maquet, the new president of the Société des Auteurs et Compositeurs Dramatiques. He seemed as well as ever when he left Maquet's house, but on his arrival at home, his servants found his lifeless body in the carriage. It was a sudden and fitting death for a man to whom life meant little outside of his work and who had been so committed to it that he left behind two comic operas, a play and an opera to be produced posthumously. An eye-witness of his funeral on February 22, described a Paris in which all business had ceased, as thousands stood bareheaded in the rain as tribute to the funeral cortege passing through the streets he had loved so well and pictured so vividly.[40]

Afterwards, the young Turks had their day, and his name was forgotten. The little *comédies-vaudevilles,* so popular in the early part of the century, disappeared and boulevard theaters were filled with the melodramas of Sardou and the social problems of Augier and Brieux. None except Sardou was grateful to Scribe, but without him, the French theater might have taken a very different turn; with him, it dominated European drama. He may not have created the great characters of Molière or the poetry of Racine, and some of his works may creak today, but we may honestly credit him with restructuring French drama and with moving it away from the sterility of neoclassic theory toward a concept of living theater still accepted and practiced today.

CHAPTER 2

Scribe and His Stage Technique

I *The Man of the Theater*

ONE of the most distinctive qualities of Scribe's work lies in its rare sensitivity to the theatrical experience. Scribe is no *littérateur* aspiring to immortality in the library, but a practicing playwright intimately concerned with the demands of the stage. This has not always worked to his advantage; critics expecting the wit of Molière, the poetry of Racine or the descriptive power of Dumas are bound to be disappointed, for his plays do not reveal their full charms on the printed page. They need the physical presence and interpretation of actors before their full impact can be felt.

The ephemeral world of the theater was no kinder to his work. Scribe wrote for repertory companies with roles well distributed among the varied talents of the players, but toward the end of his life, styles began to change and the era of the star came into being. Succeeding writers used his techniques to write the kind of vehicles particularly suited to specific performers like Bernhardt and Coquelin, strong personalities who needed only ancillary help from other players. The fashion lasted well into the twentieth century, and Scribe's work, unnoticed by critics and unplayed by theaters, faded into obscurity.

Nevertheless, the forgotten plays have retained their freshness, and their theatrical values have withstood the passage of years. In part, this is due to careful construction upon the solid foundation that is the "well-made" play. The term has been used pejoratively to indicate a formula with a standard plot, pasteboard characters and a superficial treatment. Certainly, hack writers using the formula have given impetus to criticism, but the well-made play is much more; in essence, it is a tightly knit creation that meets the requirements of theatrical representation. Scribe's skill is revealed in the very structure of his work, and his contribution lies in his simplification; all extraneous matter has been stripped away. Every character, every scene furthers the plot, rhetorical flamboyance is replaced with succinct dialogue, plot elements are foreshadowed and exploited to carry the action in a direct line from beginning to end. His method is dramatic rather than narrative; he does not describe, he demonstrates, and he is a master of the "moment."

It is true that the basic structure does not vary and once recognized can be charted in any given work. It is a leisurely presentation; in spite of some critics' declarations to the contrary, he does not plunge immediately into a crisis but rather first presents the information needed about background, situation and character. On this foundation he then erects a complex middle structure of successive crises that increase in tension until the climax is reached in what Sarcey christened the "scène à faire." This confrontation begins with the apparent downfall of the leading character and ends in his triumph. The dénouement that completes the action ties off all ends, answers remaining questions and suggests a possible future.

II Beyond Structural Innovation

Much has been written about Scribe's structural innovation, which was undeniably important to the art of the drama; but it has been emphasized at the expense of other, equally important elements in his work. Plot is crucial, and, in true Aristotelian fashion, Scribe regards the fable as the soul of the drama. Plot governs the chain of events, delineates the characters and provides the unifying factor that makes the work cohesive. Reduced to their barest essentials, most of his stories are fairly simple and seem slight in the telling, but in each case, complexities and implications are present and ready for actors' interpretations.

Scribe uses the full range of the playwright's tools, and he depends heavily on unexpected appearances, long-hidden secrets, disguises, misunderstandings and fortuitous meetings that may not have seemed as coincidental to the narrowly stratified nineteenth-century society as to that of the mobile twentieth century. People of any given class tended to frequent the same houses, cafés and spas;

it was not unusual for travellers with similar backgrounds to find that not only did they have friends in common but that they had even attended the same plays and balls. Scribe simply made use of a common phenomenon.

Aside from plot twists, variety comes from visual elements. The stage setting is no mere background for repartee or poetic passages but integral to the story. He often requires lighting and sound effects, and the bulk of his work calls for music in some form or other. The *comédies-vaudevilles* always have songs, usually well-known tunes to which he sets new lyrics, and they often end with a chorus and dance. His special contribution here was in not imposing the songs on the play but in incorporating them into the action; sometimes they further the plot, sometimes they are familiar airs that serve as commentary on the scene. He is a deft lyricist, sensitive to the rhythm of music, and his words are carefully chosen to suit the singers' needs.

Many of the early plays were strictly Parisian in topic and setting, but he soon moved to the more exotic atmosphere of the Near and Far East, Russia or America. He was fascinated with history, particularly that of the eighteenth century, which gave him the visual advantages of costumes and wigs, an advantage pursued further in his fantasies for opera and ballet. He used frequent disguises and in the early days wrote a number of "breeches" roles for women. Male attire was daring, but attractive actresses were as fond of appearing in the tight trousers of the day as their admirers were of seeing them. The comedy as a whole was enhanced by the masquerade. Stage properties are always used and often necessary to the story; food may be poisoned, elaborate screens hide secret passages, swords and guns threaten simplistic conclusions.

Most common is the ubiquitous letter. To the modern viewer, letters may seem contrived, but in an age when all communication outside the immediate vicinity had to be written, it was no more unusual than the modern dramatist's use of the telephone. Scribe's letters are read and heard with appropriate degrees of emotion, and appear in a wide variety of circumstances: in one play a missive arrives unexpectedly, in another it is lost, in a third it falls into the wrong hands.

Many of his visual effects rely on the actors' interpretation. Characters are constantly being placed in untenable situations with a choice between two equally unpalatable propositions or being prevented from achieving their desires by virtue of the very position they have painfully attained. It is here, where the elements of character and situation meet in the plot structure that Scribe's skill is most evident.

III   Character Development

It has been charged that his characters are two-dimensional, that they are indistinguishable from each other and lack greatness. Judged by the page alone, this would seem to be true, but in the theater they come to life in a remarkably rich and distinctive manner. The emphasis on plot makes his work very nearly "actor-proof," and an adequate cast will produce an enjoyable evening, while a great one will make it unforgettable. There is undoubtedly a family resemblance among his people: most plays will have an in-génue and a juvenile, a leading man and woman, a character man and woman and a servant or two—evidence of the actors available to him. Yet if their general backgrounds and motivations are familiar, the individuals are recognized by their personal histories and their present situations. There is a vast difference between the fortune hunter and the honest young man who marries a large dowry, between the protected young girl and the sophisticated miss.

He often gives characters a handicap of one sort or another. It may be a low social position or a lack of money, it may be a hostile parent or guardian, it may be physical blindness, muteness or madness. The handicap functions as a barrier to the character's desires, but it also delineates the motivations and qualities of the sufferer and his associates.

One of his most unusual techniques was the use of offstage characters, some of whom are so fully developed that they become as real as those onstage. Frequently they represent a force, hostile or benevolent, that governs the actions of the people before us; most of the time they are kept at a distance, but sometimes they are very near and may even be seen through a window or a door. They give an added dimension to the visible characters, enlarge the scope of the action and provide conflict.

Characters are lightly but clearly sketched and developed through the plot. In the early topical pieces, they are close to caricature, but as Scribe moved toward a more general comedy, they grew more realistic. The pattern, however, remained the same: once they are introduced and identified, they are faced with a series of situations demanding responses. In each case, the reaction or decision develops the character. At the finish, though they may not have changed, the audience knows them well.

They are not heroic in size but a distillation of quite ordinary qualities. Again, in an Aristotelian sense, Scribe is true to comic philosophy and paints man not as he ought to be but as he is: neither better nor worse than the average, prone to base desires but capable of nobility when that is needed. He has no classically evil characters; basically, they are decent people who respect each other, are devoted to their parents, have high moral standards and wish to improve themselves. Like all humans, they have problems, and their resolutions are not guided by high tragic moments but by the web of everyday circumstances. The bourgeois values of honesty, industry, integrity and ambition, so parallel to the Puritan values in English and American drama, are clear. Most of his people could mingle indistinguishably with the members of his audience and, indeed, allowing for differences in custom and culture, could do the same today.

IV *Language*

Scribe has also been criticised for his language, which is certainly not "poetic"; but he was first of all a playwright who understood the theatrical values of the spoken word over that of the written. He knew as well that endless emergencies arise during a performance: actors miss cues, forget lines and continually rephrase speeches. The words become secondary to the manner of delivery, and the playwright who insists on absolute fidelity to his manuscript will inevitably be disappointed. Though Scribe's lines are not witty in the literary sense, he ensured that, barring major accidents, his audience could follow the sequence of events. This approach infuriated poets who valued the word itself, and even the gentle Heine is said to have hated him. When Heine was dying, his voice began to fail, and he was asked in French if he could whistle ["siffler," meaning also "to hiss"]. He replied, with an effort, "No, not even a play by monsieur Scribe."[1]

Yet Scribe was no mere hack. He was fascinated with language and extremely sensitive to the nuances of ordinary speech; relationships are delicately established through the choice of word or phrase. He distinguishes nicely between the haute and petite bourgeoisie in speech patterns, and his ear for dialect is evident in his Swiss and Russian characters.

V *Subject*

He was, in the best sense, the playwright of the common man, and he was fascinated by the world about him. Everything was grist for his mill, from the events of the past week to the traditions of history. His ideas came from everywhere, but he imbued them with undeniable artistry and an originality entirely his own:

He had a gift of dramatic invention that perhaps no one before him had possessed: the gift of uncovering step by step, almost apropos of nothing, theatrical combinations of a new and startling effectiveness; and in uncovering them not in germ only or scarcely sketched, but in relief, in action and already before us. During the time it took his colleagues to prepare one idea, he had finished more than four; and never did he buy this prodigious fecundity at the expense of originality. His works were not cast into a banal mold . . . Not one of them but has at least a grain of novelty . . . Scribe had the genius of dramatic invention.[2]

Everything amused him, but the amusement never became contempt. He found the human condition ridiculous, but not human beings. His treatment is almost always comic, yet at the foundation is a solid belief in ideal values, and the result is comedy without a bitter aftertaste. Octave Feuillet, perhaps, said it best:

One of the most difficult arts in the domain of creativity is that of charming the imagination without shocking it, of touching the heart without troubling it, of amusing men without corrupting them. This was the supreme art of Scribe.[3]

His technique can be clearly seen in his slighter pieces, the little *comédies-vaudevilles* of his apprentice years, for it is in these that the sensitivity to audience response is most evident in topic and in treatment. They fall into four general types: topical, literary-theatrical satires, farce and serious works.

VI *Topical Works*

These were popular sketches of current events void of any pretensions to depth. Scribe is the first major playwright to use the form and to make it a valid theater piece; within five years of his first success in this *métier*, all the boulevard theaters were catering to the demand for similar works. *Une nuit de la Garde nationale*[4] was the first in a long series of plays in this mode. The plotline serves only as an excuse for the comedy of civilian-soldiers, and each incident of the story involves some comic aspect of the Guard. The Guard itself, however, is not held up to ridicule. Guardsmen, in fact, flocked to see "their" play.

Corporal Saint-Léon wants to marry the sister of Madame de Versac, who disapproves strongly of the Guard and considers it a male excuse to go out at night. Her refusal of Saint-Léon's suit is sharp, "I do not like coxcombs, and my sister feels the same. What can I do? It is a family trait." Saint-Léon's revenge is fairly innocent: he sends a false love note to her husband, supposedly an assignation from a woman Versac courted before his marriage. Versac is to go to her house, the Guard will catch him, and they will spend the night carousing, leaving the jealous wife at home alone. In the midst of their preparations, Versac himself walks in. He has promised his wife to be home every night by nine, but this evening he dined late; now he wants to be arrested and held until morning in order to provide an excuse. The captain agrees, but Madame de Versac, disguised as a man, soon appears, searching for her husband. After a number of comic situations, she realizes that her husband loves her, that the Guard is not a den of iniquity and that Saint-Léon is worthy of her sister.

The play is highly topical and very slight, but the types are universal, and the situations, delightful. Two elements are worth noting: the use of disguise for comedy and the offstage character of Madame de Versac's sister, a character intrinsic to the plot but never seen. These, along with the use of visual humor in Guardsman Pigeon's relentlessly civilian attitude, the rapid development of incidents to the climactic confrontation and the brief *dénouement*, are part of Scribe's basic technique. The current interest in the Guard no doubt gave the play its initial popularity, but the work itself is sound, the characters ring true, and the humor has not faded with the years.

Le Combat des Montagnes, ou la Folie-Beaujon was written a year later.[5] Again he treats a topical subject in an unusual manner, using classical references to symbolize a popular amusement. Folly has gone on a pilgrimage to see what has happened to Paris; all her usual haunts are empty of people. She meets the Hermit with whom she decides to build a new Olympus. He will be Momus, and, as the other characters successively appear, they also are cast as gods: The Actress, Hortensia (Venus); Calicot, the soldier-like merchant (Mercury); Antimèche, the lampmaker who wants to illuminate all Paris with a single gigantic lamp fueled with hydrogen (Apollo); a restaurateur (Comus); a hunchback locksmith (Vulcan); and the cashier of the Odéon (Pluto). A Titan represents the entrepreneur of the "Russian mountains," that is, a roller coaster, then other "mountains" appear, singing their own praises. The Titans unite in a battle against the gods, but, true to mythic history, the Olympians win.

The mythological echoes are not in the least esoteric, and the "gods" are reflections of the day. The epic overtones in the battle lend an edge to the comedy by an implicit comparison between past and present society. Neither classically idealized nor satirically debased, they are realistic human types with familiar motivations. Never once does Scribe sharpen his humor into the "sacred lance" of the satirist claiming to be improving morals. The clerks who took umbrage at the character of Calicot were hypersensitive to ridicule, for clearly there is no attempt to point a finger at their soldierly costumes. Scribe's comedy is in the situation, not the individuals.

L'Hôtel des Quatre Nations[6] celebrates the removal of foreign troops from French soil after the reparation payments of 1818. Lefranc, the owner of the hotel, is a permanent optimist, but he wishes to marry his daughter, Juliette, to a prosperous paper merchant, Velouté, a permanent pessimist. Velouté agrees because the hotel is thriving, but Juliette thinks only of Sans-Régret, now away in the army. In the beginning there are four residents in the hotel; suddenly, they are all called away, and Velouté, certain that Lefranc is ruined, refuses to marry Juliette. At this moment, Sans-Régret returns from the army, and the play closes with a four-nation chorus, each national touting his own country while agreeing that France is best.

Each of the hotel clients is a symbolic representative of his country as seen through French eyes. Each is defined by accent and personality: the Englishman speaks incorrect French interlarded with English words like "Goddam" and thinks of suicide; the German reverses "p" for "b" and "f" for "v" and has coarse manners; Sonikoff, the Russian, speaks good French (but his servant's is abominable) and spends all his time making love to Juliette. There is no plot reason for Sonikoff to be played by a woman, but, since almost every scene has music, it is possible that Scribe wanted the vocal balance of Madame Cuisot's contralto, particularly evident in the final chorus.

A slight work of no lasting value, it is interesting, nonetheless, for its use of theatrical devices. The action never falters, the characters contrast and balance, the situations are amusing, and the climax is joyous and satisfying. It is, perhaps, one of the clearest demonstrations of Scribe's amiability; not even toward the enemies of France does he display animosity.

Such works as these are not masterpieces, but they served as an apprenticeship in the difficult art of dramatic writing. Whether the theme is as profound as *Oedipus* or as light as farce, the demands of the stage remain constant; within a limited time, the playwright must create a believable world peopled with characters consistent with its premise, must capture and maintain the attention of the audience, and must leave them with a sense of satisfaction. Scribe learned his craft quickly, for the uninhibited Parisian audience left no doubt as to whether or not it was pleased, and the lessons proved valuable as he matured.

VII   *Literary-Theatrical Satires*

A second, concurrent, mode was the satire of contemporary literary and theatrical fare. Scribe, unable to scourge his fellow man, regarded artistic abuses with acidity. Sometimes he used symbolic terms, sometimes realistic, but in every case the humor was devastatingly accurate. He does not focus on a specific personality but on general practices, and the point is turned against audiences, managers and performers alike. It is the comedy of a clever young writer, amused and annoyed by stale tradition and secondrate work.

One of the earliest of these is *Flore et Zéphyre*[7] which requires an unusually large cast of ten men and seven women. Although some of the references to current repertory might be lost today, the visual humor overrides the language and the showy piece is still good entertainment.

Grand-Opéra wants to marry off his daughter, Flore, but she loves Zéphyre who has been banished. Suitors arrive one by one: Demetrius, who complains that he wants to rise but cannot because the public prefers his brother Artaxerxes who is better; an inventor of a mechanical giant and giantess, two jugglers and an Englishman whose sole talent is that he walks. At last, Zéphyre, who has become a great dancer, returns to win Flore in a final extravagant chorus and dance.

The play reflects Scribe's intimate knowledge of backstage life. One dancer complains of fatigue after a night on the town, another of asthma; the box office man is an expert in ticket scalping. Many of the characters have symbolic names, but they are patently human and their motivations are the familiar love, hate, greed, ambition, etc. The plot is negligible, and aside from the scene of Demetrius's complaints with its satire of the wildly popular tragedy, *Artaxerxes*, the comedy is almost entirely visual.

Most important, however, is the statement that true worth, which wins out is the only quality worth having in life or art. As in most of Scribe's work, great care has been taken not to let the "message" dominate the action. Here he has presented such a variety of personalities and situations that the entertainment value overshadows the serious core. This very same skill often blinded superficial critics to the essentially serious foundation on which he built his farcical plots.

Similar to *Flore et Zéphyre* is *Wallace, ou la Barrière Mont-Parnasse*.[8] More symbolic than its predecessor, it contains even less plot; its humor lies almost entirely in visual effects and topical references.

At the gates of Mount Parnassus, the sentry Halte-Là guards the way against secondrate art. Fanchette and Thibaut, two characters from *Les Deux Jaloux*, announce that a great Scottish character, Wallace, will be arriving and should not be stopped. An amateurish flute player is barred and goes away. Macbeth arrives on a white horse and jumps the barrier. A dancer is allowed through after she performs before a huge mirror—actually two dancers in a mirror routine. Dogueman brings his Italian "genius" poodle, Munito, but is refused admission when the dog does absolutely nothing. They pass the barrier when Munito darts through and Dogueman chases him. At last, Wallace appears, accompanied by Robert Bruce as a drummer boy, but he is not allowed to pass—despite the pleas of Fanchette and Thibaut—until he produces the musical score of his play. The grand finale is a performance of this score.

Here Scribe plays on the combination of the Parisian Montparnasse and the classical Parnassus, home of the arts. Admission to the celestial regions is supposedly permitted only to genius, but it is clear that the barrier may be passed by any determined trickster. It is thus equally clear that true worth is not always recognized.

Though the tone is mocking and the darts thrown at current favorites are sharp, the victims are always plays. Never does Scribe descend to personal invective.

The plot, such as it is, functions in an important fashion to prevent the series of specialties from becoming merely a parade sequence; each, amusing in itself, builds toward Wallace's entrance and, while demonstrating what should not be admitted to Parnassus, implicitly indicates what should be allowed. It is a curious piece of sharp criticism made palatable by humor.

Les Trois Genres,[9] a more ambitious effort than the foregoing, and uses a "frame-plot" as a setting for the body of the work. It is a virtuoso piece, demonstrating Scribe's skill in uniting three disparate modes into a unified entertainment which included a full musical score. The music was by Auber, who had the year before written the scores for Scribe's *Leicester* and *Le Neige,* and Boieldieu, who would compose *La Dame blanche* a year later.

The frame concerns d'Herbelin, a stay-at-home currently angry with the Odéon for producing a play based on a ridiculous incident in his own life. His friend, Simon, persuades him to visit the theaters on a rehearsal night so that he may avoid crowds yet have an evening tailored to his taste: an act of tragedy at the Théâtre-Français, one of comedy at the Salle Feydeau and music at the Opéra-Comique. After they leave, d'Herbelin's niece, Fanchette, reveals that she has been engaged for second leads at the Odéon, and leaves for rehearsal. The two men supposedly arrive at the Français where they watch scenes of tragedy and comedy. Suddenly, an *opéra-comique* begins. Fanchette is discovered and so is Simon's plot: he has brought d'Herbelin to the Odéon.

The frame sets a comic premise in d'Herbelin's insistent dislike of the Odéon, the very theater in which the play was being given. The three interludes are not only inherently interesting as examples of contemporary taste, but are delightful commentaries on the three forms. The frame is typically Scribean in that it serves the dual function of unifying the separate scenes and of providing an extra plot interest in the relationship of d'Herbelin, Simon and the stage-struck Fanchette. Her character is a delicious satire of the ambitious actress who, having at last won a coveted position in a professional company, becomes at once dissatisfied with second leads and aspires to stardom. The scene in which she fumbles her one line may be Scribe's way of punishing such self-aggrandisement, but as always, he forgives her and she stays in the company. Simon's

deception of d'Herbelin involves a remarkable piece of craftsmanship; without the slightest confusion to the audience, the play
moves from house to theater, from frame to genre and back, maintaining at all times a complete believability in both the overall story
and in the excerpts from the plays.

Farinelli, ou la Pièce de circonstance,[10] is a more realistic treatment of the artistic error than Flore et Zéphyre or Wallace. Here,
Scribe ridicules the callousness with which many of his contemporaries seized on topical events for their plays. The treatment is
light, but the underpinning is serious and the values humanistic.

Farinelli, a famous Italian singer, is vacationing in a Parisian
hotel under the name Spinoletto. Like all singers, he is tempera-
mental and eats only apples, a delicacy much coveted by the porter,
who steals them for himself. Two would-be authors, l'Affut and
l'Eclair, also help themselves as they work out their idea for a new
play based on a newspaper report that Farinelli is dead. Since they
know nothing of Italy or the singer, they ask "Spinoletto" for help.
There follows an amusing scene satirizing popular vaudevilles as
created by inept writers. When Farinelli realizes what they are doing and also that they have finished his apples, he revenges himself
by telling them the apples were poisoned, and, as they think they
are dying, pretends to take notes for a vaudeville of his own "based
on two authors dying of poison." When they have learned their
lesson, the truth is told and the ending is cheerful for all.

Not too many of the audience might have been familiar with the
original Farinelli, the eighteenth-century castrato singer idolized
throughout Europe, but Scribe seems to have been fascinated by his
career. In 1857 he published a novel, Carlo Broschi (Farinelli's real
name), based on the singer's life. He was clearly aware of Farinelli's
operatic career, and in the tradition of that medium, designed the
role for a woman. He also used historical facts for comic purposes—l'Eclair reads of an incident in the Gazette:

The prince had fallen into a black melancholy; he no longer presided over
the council and he even neglected his person to the point of letting his
beard grow. The princess placed the young Farinelli at the door of his
apartment; she ordered him to sing one of his most beautiful airs. Scarcely
had he finished than the distracted prince, transported with pleasure, ran to
him, embraced him and swore to grant his slightest wish. "Well," answered
Farinelli, "I ask that your Highness dress himself and go to the council." In
that moment began the favor he never lost.

It appears a fantastic legend invented for the occasion, but it actually happened in Spain. The king was Philip V, and the real Farinelli was retained as court singer for twenty-five years.[11] However, a knowledge of the history is not necessary for enjoyment of the play; still, an awareness of the facts enriches the comedy.

Like the topical pieces, the satires are exercises in the playwright's craft. They are limited by too close a relationship to contemporary events, as even Scribe admitted in his introduction to *Le Combat des montagnes:* "Parodies and circumstantial pieces are essentially the domain of vaudeville. Unhappily, they rarely survive beyond the event that brought them into being." Nevertheless, they display, perhaps more clearly than works of greater depth, those elements that make an effective experience in the theater.

VIII *Farce*

A group of these light works is not topical, though the settings and themes were currently popular in drama and literature. These are primarily farcical, but some satiric elements are present, and the moral emphasis is unmistakable.

The writer of farce is permitted a wider range of probability in constructing his work than even the writer of comedy; indeed, the farce writer is expected to use coincidence, exaggeration and unusual turns of plot. The humor lies in the unlikely premise, unusual characters or the impossible success snatched from the ashes of disaster. Scribe's gift for the unexpected was of great advantage here, and he used it to create works still amusing almost two centuries after their debuts.

His earliest farce, *Les Dervis*,[12] was not a success. It has, however, a surprising sophistication, considering the authors were no more than twenty years of age. Three Frenchmen, slaves of a Cadi, have disguised themselves as "dervishes" in order to escape. Lelio, however, wants to rescue Isabelle, a captive Frenchwoman he loves, as well. With the help of his servant and a Turkish slave, the Cadi is secretly brought to them on the pretext that they can make Isabelle fall in love with him. They acquaint Isabelle with their plans, and all escape with a goodly share of the Cadi's gold.

Although dervishes were supposedly the Islamic version of pious mendicant friars, Scribe treats them as if they were suspect to ordinary Mohammedans, rather like practitioners of the black mass. Part of the comedy actually lies in the secrecy the Cadi demands for his visit. The humor is visual: the exotic setting of "Scutari, near Constantinople," the disguises and the false magic show by which they "prove" their power by revealing the Cadi's other illegal activities—knowledge they have gained as his slaves. A modern touch comes when the Cadi is reluctant to let Isabelle meet privately with the dervishes as they insist; she threatens him with "Listen, Sir Cadi, nothing is more dangerous than denying me what I want—tomorrow I shall have a headache."[13] It is thoroughly enjoyable froth, but so carefully structured that it is almost impossible to omit a single speech without irreparable damage to the plot.

L'Ours et le Pacha[14] was written nine years later. Set in the same general location as Les Dervis, it shows considerable advancement in technique and maintains a more farcical premise without faltering. The basic story is no more complicated than in the earlier play, but the characterizations and intrigues are greatly developed. It became an immediate favorite, remained in the repertory for years, and in 1870 was posthumously revived as an opéra-comique with music by Bazin.

In this play, the pasha's polar bear has died, and his chief eunuch, Ali, is afraid to tell him, for the pasha is an impulsive ruler with a quick temper and likely to behead the nearest person when he hears bad news. When two poverty stricken French adventurers arrive, one, Tristapatte, discovers his wife, Roxelane, had been kidnapped and is now the pasha's favorite. The other, Lagingeole, is a true charlatan. He tells Ali they have a black bear to sell (actually an unwilling Tristapatte inside a bear's skin), and a demonstration of the "bear's" dancing and flute-playing delights the pasha so much that he insists Lagingeole teach the polar bear the same tricks. Fearing the pasha's anger, Ali dons the white bearskin, and a very funny scene follows, in which Ali and Tristapatte, neither of whom knows the other is not a real bear, meet and try to escape from each other. In the confusion, the bearheads fall off—but their relief is only momentary, for the pasha approaches. Quickly, they re-don the heads—but in the confusion put on the wrong ones, and the pasha finally realizes the truth. He decides one must lose his head and tries to make Roxelane choose which; but when she cannot, he orders both beheaded. The men lay their bearheads at his feet, and the pasha, amused, allows the French couple to be reunited and to depart with Lagingeole, richer by twelve thousand sequins.

The visual humor in the plot is evident. But there is verbal humor as well, as when an intense argument develops over whether a fillip on the nose should be called a *"croquignole,"* a *"pichenette"* or a *"chiquenaude."* One of the most striking examples of Scribe's increased skill is in the way he achieves his happy ending; the "impossible choice" presented to Roxelane leads directly to the symbolic but unexpected "beheading," and the pasha's pardon. That this sudden change is acceptable is clearly a development of Scribe's dramatic powers.

Of particular interest is the character Lagingeole, the manipulator of people and events. A rudimentary *"raisonneur,"* who brings about the successful conclusion by his cleverness, his type goes back beyond the time of the medieval Pierre Pathelin. Scribe gives him a new moral respectability, for Lagingeole's cleverness is not directed solely toward selfish ends. By using his wits to help his friends, he ceases to be merely a calculating fraud and becomes a valuable ally who serves the ultimate good and is even rewarded. His is a character who appears frequently in the later social comedies.

Le Valet de son rival[15] does not rely on an exotic setting for its humor, but was a favorite with Parisians also. The story concerns Senneville, who has come to Strasbourg on a diplomatic mission. He arrives at d'Estival's house by mistake to find himself mistaken for Beauclair, to whom d'Estival plans to marry his daughter. When the true Beauclair arrives, he acts as Senneville's valet, according to an earlier agreement they had once made when their situations were reversed. As "Jasmine," the valet, Beauclair tries to undermine Senneville's character by false descriptions of wild escapades, but when all is revealed, Senneville is the winner and Beauclair is sent away.

Here the setting allows for a certain amount of humor at the expense of provincials, and the mistaken identity theme is turned and turned again until d'Estival cannot tell Senneville from Beauclair; yet the audience is never confused. The play involves a game of wits in which the antagonists are so evenly matched that it is impossible to predict who will win. Senneville, however, has a distinct advantage because he had met Lise six months earlier, had fallen in love and remained true to her. The prognosis of such an attachment is invariably optimistic in these farces, for Scribe disapproves of the loveless arranged marriage and of thoughtless passion equally.

Le Parrain[16], like *Le Valet de son rival*, is one of the few one-act comedies without music; it provided the comedian, Perlet, with an excellent stellar role as the reluctant godfather. Monsieur Godard's wife has just had a son and the christening approaches. He has chosen his banker's wife, Madame de Saint-Ange, as the godmother—and his tenant, Durand—as the godfather. Durand hates the idea and is persuaded only after Madame de Saint-Ange says her husband will help him with his investments; but he is distracted by the duties and expense of his new responsibility. Meanwhile, the Count de Holden asks the midwife, Prudent, to care for his newborn daughter while he arranges family matters; somehow the babies are switched, and after the christening, the "son" is found to be a daughter. The Count returns and straightens out the problem, but another christening must now take place, and Durand is again impressed into service. At the curtain, he vows to marry and make Godard godfather to all his children.

Though mistaken identity here is given a novel twist in the mixup of the infants, the main humor centers on the character of the egocentric Durand. To Scribe, his type was a proper target for ridicule; and Durand describes himself with fine irony:

I never sought a position, for fear of the work, so I do nothing; I never bought property, for fear of inconvenience, so I remain single. I have 12,000 francs a year. I am entertained by everyone without entertaining anybody, because a bachelor is not obliged to entertain. For the rest, I am a good citizen, I pay my taxes . . . . It isn't that I'm a miser, I'm just careful; I spend my income generously, but I have made it a rule not to spend a penny for the pleasure of anyone but myself. I live alone, I dine alone, I sleep alone, and it is on myself alone that I have concentrated my dearest affections.[17]

The other device especially worth noting is in the use of offstage characters. Here they are more than atmosphere, for Monsieur de Saint-Ange is the prime motivating force in Durand's behavior, while the Countess de Holden is responsible for the mixup of the babies. Each is given an identity and a function within the total action.

Le Solliciteur, ou l'Art d'obtenir des places[18] is also a farce with the satiric edge directed toward the machinations of the ambitious. Armand, an apprentice in the ministry, wants an official appointment, and his friend, Madame de Versac, is trying to see the minister on his behalf. The main character is Lespérance, a professional office seeker who dodges the Swiss guard, attempts bribery, disguises himself and finally delivers the secretary's lunch in an effort to gain a license for a tobacco shop. He succeeds in seeing the minister, but, unfortunately for him, the minister signs the wrong petition and Armand is appointed an inspector. Lespérance goodhumoredly accepts the situation and starts over again.

Again Scribe motivates the action and the climax by means of offstage characters in a skillful piece of planning: Madame de Versac furiously reports that her hopes for Armand are dashed, for the minister will see only three people this day, a general, a duchess and Monsieur de la Ribardière. It is a comic scene, and the names of the three pass almost unnoticed; only later, when Lespérance describes his scene in the minister's waitingroom, does the last name become significant:

At last the usher announced in a stentorian voice, "Monsieur de la Ribardière!" Our man tried to raise himself from the armchair in whch, so to speak, he had taken root. Burdened with his umbrella, his sword and his cough, he fell back feebly into the chair. I didn't lose a moment; while he was collecting himself, I shot like an arrow into the minister's office and had already made two or three bows before he was standing again.[19]

The character of Lespérance, played by Potier, the Vaudeville's chief comedian, is outstanding; with "audacity and slenderness," he claims, one can achieve anything, and much of the humor is centered on his various schemes to gain his ends.

Scribe pokes fun at the political and governmental system, but the work is not a wholesale condemnation. Rather, it is an amusing commentary on the way things are; the way they ought to be is implicit in the values expressed, but there is no indication that the ideal is possible or even desirable, for the focus remains on the comic elements of human behavior.

Like *Le Solliciteur*, *La Manie des places, ou la Folie du siècle*[20] is close to satire. But here too, while he pokes fun at the mania for prestige, he accepts folly as a part of the human condition rather than as a sin in need of corrosive correction. The play is set in a hotel where a cross-section of society meets; the emphasis is not on status, but on those qualities, good and bad, that are common to all.

Frederic has come to Paris looking for the father of the girl he loves, Monsieur de Berlac. Berlac, having gone mad after being refused a position in the government, in his madness thinks he is an appointee. The position varies from time to time, but at present he thinks he is a minister. In a series of farcical scenes, the local inhabitants, who believe Berlac, besiege him with applications for places. At last, they learn the truth, but Frederic, who soothes their indignation, is rewarded witih Berlac's daughter. Berlac, now convinced he is an ambassador, agrees that the newlyweds should travel with him to his new "station."

The characters are types, individualized in their own desires and ambitions and clearly drawn as in the portrayal of their reactions to the false minister. The most unusual aspect, perhaps, is in Berlac's madness; in an age when insanity was either a matter for laughter or proof of moral collapse, Scribe is sympathetic. The ending is gentle, for no one ridicules Berlac, and Frederic says he and his bride will maintain the fictional ambassadorship until Berlac is cured. The mania is amusing in its effect on others but not in itself, nor is it evidence of an evil soul. Rather, it is poignant, and if there is a villain, it is the system that has driven Berlac to his extreme condition.

Les Empiriques d'autrefois[21] was a long-time favorite. The reason is not difficult to divine, for the play is an hilàrious farce built about a common human trait and replete with amusing scenes.

Gaspard and Robert are charlatans, driven from the previous town because they had frightened the villagers by writing on walls with phosphorescent paint and pretending to be magicians. They have picked up Pedrillo, a young soldier who wants to visit the present village because he grew up here and fell in love. To repair their empty purses, the two charlatans claim they can raise the dead and offer to bring back the recently deceased village mayor, planning to sell tickets to the event. Tuffiador, the new mayor, offers them a sizable amount of money to forget their plan; and, realizing the value of their new project, Gaspard sends Robert through the village offering to bring back friends and relatives and collecting large sums from those who don't want them back. Of all the villagers, only Estelle wants someone to return; being forced to marry Gregorio, a lumpish farmer, she really loves Pedrillo, believed dead. As Gaspard promises to raise Pedrillo, a good deal of suspicion arises among the villagers, and the charlatans are required to perform their miracle. Before them all, Gaspard "returns" Pedrillo from the dead, the lovers are reunited, the village has its money's worth of show, and the entrepreneurs retire from the scene, prosperous once more.

The action takes place in sixteenth-century Spain, in Don Quixote's own province of La Mancha, but the historical setting in no way dates the action, for the story could with equal credibility be set in a small twentieth-century town. The use of a past age softens the satire, but the distance in time does not diminish the insight on human behavior. At the same time, the visual elements are enhanced by colorful costumes.

This time, Scribe uses an unusual offstage character, for the former mayor is dead; his spirit, however, provides the basis for the action and the response of the characters. Another familiar technique is in the pairing of the charlatans; as in *l'Ours et le pacha*, the doubling serves several purposes simultaneously: it allows a casual mode of exposition and a fine contrast of the two types. Gaspard and Robert are two individuals whose motivations are entirely dissimilar; Robert is uneducated, a charlatan "by trade" and skilled in his craft; Gaspard, the trained doctor expelled from his profession because he actually tried to cure his patients, has vision and originality which make him a charlatan "by philosophy." Tricksters who prey on the lesser aspects of man, they are also kind and unselfish. We admire their cleverness and applaud their results. Like many French writers, Scribe respects cleverness and does not deplore the manipulation of others if the end is acceptable. Yet it is not simply that the end justifies the means, for there are restrictions: the manipulator must not be self-seeking, no one must be hurt in the process and the end must be of general benefit. The adventurers of *Les Empiriques d'autrefois* meet all these requirements.

Scribe's farces are noteworthy not only for their exploitation of theatrical devices, but for the originality with which these are used. Disguises, mistaken identity, misdirected letters, offstage personalities and comic accents are the stock in trade of most farceurs. Scribe, however, weaves them into the direct line of action in a manner few have been able to master. The disguises of *l'Ours et le pacha* are more than a device, for they bring about the *dénouement;* the mistaken identity in *Le Valet de Son rival* is the heart of the plot itself. In utilizing such effects as integral to the structure, Scribe enhances both; the result is comedy that remains fresh and novel.

IX *Serious Plays*

Although Scribe is primarily known for comedy, and the bulk of his work is in that vein, he also wrote more serious works. Most were less effective and have been largely ignored by critics and actors alike. They are, however, valuable from a technical point of view, for the mechanics are more visible, and the skeleton, unfleshed by comic situation, is easily examined. It is here that Scribe betrays his allegiance to his own time, for while the skill is evident, the tone is often too sentimental for later tastes.

In a day when melodrama was still in good repute, *Les Frères invisibles*[22] was announced as a "melodrama in three acts." It exemplifies the term, for the plot is worthy of grand opera. Salvator, under the name Léonce, is at Ragusa to protect the people from brigands who depredate the countryside. Actually, until now, the brigand leader has been Salvator himself, but he has fallen in love with Camille and reformed. They are to be married, but dire warnings against the wedding are· given by mysterious voices; Salvator defies the voices and his brigand band to marry Camille. The outlaws kidnap her, and he leads the soldiers to find her and extirpate them, but he cannot free himself from his oath of loyalty to them. Camille is rescued, the outlaw band broken, and Salvator dies.

It is a fine example of Scribe's "impossible situation," for the basic action puts Salvator into such a position, that he is constantly torn between his love for Camille and his loyalty to the outlaws. There is a hint of the supernatural in the mysterious voices (although they are eventually explained), and in the fate theme that finally destroys Salvator. The outstanding quality, however, is in the stage effects: the exotic Italian setting, the ominous offstage voices and bells, and the confrontation in a subterranean cave; even the contrasting costumes of the wedding guests and the brigands are unusually colorful.

Melodrama is a curious mode. It produces an intense experience, often effective in the playhouse, but its lasting quality is even more fragile than that of comedy; this is a basic weakness of the form. Comic characters can be delineated by situation, but serious figures need more personal definition. Scribe's writing here is as skillful as in his farces, but the nature of melodrama makes it less appealing to an age that uses another set of conventions for the same intensified experience.

X *Sentimental Plays*

In contrast to the melodramas, the sentimental one-acts have maintained their charm. This mode, a theatrical staple from the mideighteenth century to daytime television, can be painfully trite, but Scribe's gift for plot variations precludes banality. The sentimental play is usually a simple love story in which the principal lovers are kept separated until the last moment, when the presumably insurmountable barriers are removed. For most playwrights of the time, the barrier involved either social position or money, and a deus-ex-machina in the form of a long-lost relative or a sudden inheritance usually resolved the problem. Scribe's love stories provide only the foundation on which to develop widely variant plots and characters. Everyday events form the basis of action, yet the characters, simple in appearance, are subtly drawn. Their motivations and backgrounds incorporate fundamental drives with occasionally surprising implications.

Michel et Christine[23] has a simple plot with only four characters in a single setting against a common phenomenon, war. The main theme, however, concerns not death but survival. Stanislas, a soldier who has been given a fortune by a dying colonel, returns to the inn where he was once given a much needed drink of water by Christine, a young orphan. Now that he has some resources, he wants to marry her and settle down, but he finds she loves Michel, who is away and believed dead. When Michel reappears, Stanislas gives them his blessing, money, and goes back to the army.

The characterizations are of the utmost importance, and the three main roles are deceptive in their apparent simplicity. All three are romantic, but with an admirable dollop of *"raison,"* the common sense which prevents sentimentality. Each has dignity, integrity and charm, and if their social status is low, their principles are not. Christine exemplifies a favorite type of Scribean woman, independent, industrious and kind. Through sheer hard work she has raised herself from kitchen slavey to owner of a prosperous inn, and her qualities reveal the reason for her success. She is both frugal and generous—she wastes nothing but is always ready to help the needy.

Michel has the same qualities but is even more unusual. To most Parisians, a provincial was a figure of fun, but Scribe carefully noted, "This character should not be played as foolish; that would destroy the entire effect of the work,"[24] and pointed to Perlet's renowned performances of similar characters in other plays. Michel emerges as a "pure" love, unsophisticated and uncorrupted by experience but wise in the ways of the heart.

Stanislas is, perhaps, the most romantic of the three and the most interesting. His love for Christine may be counted as genuine, for it is no sudden passion (always suspect to Scribe), but a years-long memory that draws him back to her. Loyalty, gratitude and courage add to his military glamour; his quixotic gesture in giving her his small fortune leaves him no alternative but to return to the army. His abandonment of Christine to Michel is true romantic heroism. Characteristically, this resolution is touched with practicality, for it is obvious that Michel will be the more steady mate and he loves her deeply.

Not being a drama of tragic intensity, the impact lies in the depiction of ordinary people in ordinary situations, who, in their daily lives perform the noblest of actions. Scribe, however, was evidently not satisfied with Stanislas' sacrifice, for he wrote two sequels.

The first, simply titled *Stanislas*,[25] transports the scene to Poland seven years later, where Michel and Christine, who still have their inn, have saved enough to repay Stanislas. They revere his memory, especially Christine's sister, Pauleska, who dresses and speaks in military fashion. She is to marry a cowardly farmer, Griff. A battle is going on offstage, and Stanislas appears with a rescued child, learns Pauleska's identity, and they fall in love. Stanislas, hearing of her proposed marriage, again plans to leave, giving half his money to the child, half for Pauleska's dowry; but she locates the child's father (Stanislas's colonel!) and obtains permission for them to marry. The happy ending has Griff going off to learn soldiering.

The play has some amusing scenes, especially those with Griff, but as a whole it does not match *Michel et Christine* in depth. Scribe, too, may not have approved of it, for two months later *Le Retour, ou la Suite de Michel et Christine*[26] made its debut. Set in France, it incorporates more skillfully some of the elements in *Stanislas*. Again Christine has a sister, but "Lisa" is not grotesquely military; there is no fiancé, but a little of Griff's cowardice seems to have rubbed off on Michel, who has taken advantage of a supposedly fatal accident to avoid conscription. Stanislas pursues the "widowed" Christine, but when the misunderstandings are cleared, he proposes to Lisa; and this time he really wants to settle down.

Here the ordinarily forbidden love-at-first-sight is justified because Lisa is so like her sister. Again, the admirable qualities of Michel and Christine are revealed in practical terms: they had sold the inn at a profit several years previously and are now successful farmers; a neighboring farm, purchased earlier and maintained for Stanislas, in fact, becomes his wedding gift. The atmosphere and characters of this play are more consistent with the original than the more raffish humor of *Stanislas*, and as a sequel retains the delicate charm of the original.

Scribe's short pieces have markedly dissimilar plots and situations. One quite unlike any other is *Rodolphe, ou Frère et soeur*,[27] another small cast in a single setting. The story is evenly balanced among the characters. Rodolphe, a former sailor, is in love with Thérèse, a young orphan whom he rescued from her dying mother and has brought up as his sister. He thinks she loves his partner, Antoine, a clever businessman who has made them both rich and who now wants to marry her. Thérèse is not in love with Antoine but agrees to obey her brother, until Louise, Antoine's sister, describes her own feelings for the young man she is going to marry. At this point, Thérèse realizes her feelings for Rodolphe are not sisterly. It is only when all the truth is told that she can marry him.

Though on the surface it seems mere sentiment, the play deals with complex human questions. Rodolphe is torn by the familiar conflict between intellect and emotion; rationally he thinks a marriage between his old friend and his ward would be ideal, but the reality throws him into a violent rage against both of them. He does not recognize the cause of his anger because he thinks of himself as a kind of parent, because he adores Thérèse, and because he does not believe himself worthy of her love. The resolution brings to him, as it does to Thérèse, a clearer knowledge of self. Antoine's generosity in relinquishing Thérèse when he realizes the true state of affairs, is akin to Stanislas's sacrifice; but the circumstances are so different as to be quite new. The least colorful character, Louise, is responsible for the most dramatic scene in the play, for her description of love leads to Thérèse's realization of her own feelings. Although the audience is fully aware of the relationship to Rodolphe, the implication of incest is unmistakable. Scribe therefore treads on very thin ice. Only his ability to keep the audience from stopping to reflect keeps the comic thread intact.

The theme of sacrifice frequently occurs throughout his work, and in *Le Mauvais Sujet*[28] it appears again. The play has the charm but little of the humor found in *Michel et Christine*, for the topic is more serious and the treatment distinctly moral. Gervais, a prosperous village notary, wants his daughter Estelle to marry Raymond, a wealthy young businessman who has grown up with her. In contrast to his older brother, Robert, Raymond is steady and industrious—and he loves Estelle. She, however, still loves Robert, although he ran away in disgrace years before. The repentant Robert, now a sailor, returns unrecognized, still in love with Estelle and hoping to regain his former life. When he realizes how badly he has hurt his family and friends and that he has little to offer Estelle, he persuades her to marry Raymond and goes away again.

There is some comedy in the character of Isidore, a grasping young farmer who wants to marry Estelle because of her dowry, but as a whole the play is sober in tone; Robert's sacrifice suggests that even though an individual may be rehabilitated, he must pay for his errors. As always with Scribe, events move rapidly once the preparation is over; he maintains the suspense through the disguise, penetrated at once by the audience but never by the characters. The happy ending is achieved at a price only the audience knows, giving a poignant turn to Robert's penance and to the marriage as well.

Scribe seldom adapted existing literary works for the stage; most of his ideas came from the world about him. Occasionally, however, he would adapt a dramatic story—which in his hands would undergo a noticeable transformation. Such a work was Charles Nodier's *Trilby, ou le Lutin d'Argail*, which first appeared in 1822. Scribe's changes are considerable. Nodier's story concerns Jeannie, a young Scottish woman married to the fisherman, Dougal. Trilby, a magical goblin figure in the form of a child, loves her and visits her in dreams. When she tells Dougal, he brings a priest to exorcise the spirit, and the results are most unpleasant. Dougal no longer catches the fine large fish he had formerly, and Jeannie, who begins to dream of Trilby as a handsome young man, is haunted by guilt.

Scribe uses the basic elements of Nodier's story, but alters the outline and the emphasis.[29] His Jeannie is the unmarried goddaughter of Mother Dougal, a poor cottager. A poor young orphan from a good family she is about to marry Job Mac-Lof, secretary to the Count Athol. Trilby falls in love with her and sends letters threatening Mother Dougal and Mac-Lof if they force Jeannie to marry. They persuade Jeannie to send Trilby away forever; she does and is wretched. Then Arthur, the Count's son, arrives; he too loves Jeannie and has at last obtained his father's permission to marry her. She accepts, and the end is happy.

Here Scribe uses visual elements to great advantage. The scene is romantic—a simple cottage in Scotland where villagers are imbued with highland mysticism, and where a sprite like Trilby seems a part of the natural setting. The highland costume, as exotic to a Parisian audience as the Turkish or Chinese dress, adds to the strangeness, as does Trilby's unearthly appearance and behavior.

If the play lacks some of the delicacy of the Nodier tale, it has something more important in the theater—dramatic impact. Nodier leaves the reader to wonder if Trilby is supernatural or a sexual image from Jeannie's unconscious; Scribe's version is equally ambiguous but presented in stage terms: Trilby/Arthur is played by the same person. The disparity between the two characters gave Minette-Laforest an opportunity for a virtuoso performance as the mischievous dancing spirit and as the serious young lover, but the very fact that one player portrayed both raises questions: is the "spirit" really Arthur in disguise, playing a capricious joke to test Jeannie's love? Is Arthur really Trilby returned to claim his love? Or is the Trilby sequence a product of Jeannie's imagination, an unconscious revolt against her approaching marriage to Mac-Lof? The theatrical time-stream allows no time for speculation, but a director would need to think carefully before beginning rehearsals, for the play is so nicely balanced that a commitment to any one answer alters the concept of the whole.

Scribe, of course, had neither the advantages of twentieth-century stage technology nor the flexibility of the camera available to him. He did, however, have the three basic elements of any good theater: actors, audience and platform. These he utilized fully and provided later theaters with a body of works that lend themselves equally to the simplest or most elaborate staging.

His plays reveal a sensitivity to the stage unique among playwrights who never acted. It is evident that the stories of his constant attendance at rehearsals and performances, his careful revisions before (but never after!) the plays opened, and his close companionship with the players were not exaggerated. Certainly few playwrights of any age have displayed such awareness of contemporary style or had greater control of the genre.

His emphasis on visual and audial effects has prevented his plays from affecting literary critics as deeply as they did his contemporary audiences, and his dialogue, created to be spoken, does not read as well as that of lesser dramatists more conscious of the written word. But in his structure, his endless variations of plot, his colloquial language and his knowledge of audience reaction, he clearly had mastered the art of the theater.

CHAPTER 3

The Social Comedies

I *Social Conditions*

DURING most of Scribe's life, the social milieu was unsettled. Although the *ancien régime* ended four years before he was born, it did not entirely vanish. The republican era of his growing years came to a close with the downfall of Napoleon, and the monarchies that followed revived the vestiges of the old aristocracy. As its descendents tried to reestablish their claims politically and socially, a new aristocracy, based on wealth, grappled for power. The fluctuating center was reflected not only in the breakdown of the old hierarchy, but also in the shifting of values. When birth no longer determined nobility, the quality of individual behavior became important, no longer measured by centuries-long tradition but by the moral standards of the majority, the bourgeoisie.

Scribe's loyalties are firmly fixed with the new ruling class, and his social comedies deal with their concerns. Superficially, most of his plays may appear to be simple love stories with happy endings, but often the love interest is merely the unifying element of the plot, used to focus attention as the theme develops, for he covers a broad spectrum of questions. He is concerned with honor in the moral, not chivalric, sense and his "good" characters may come from any social level. The truly noble person, whether stockbroker, artist or viscount, has a rigorous standard of integrity. He cares for others and will sacrifice his own ambition and desire for the welfare of a fellow creature, even one who may not deserve it. He has a sense of duty, particularly toward the family, for which all personal considerations are brushed aside. This seeming paragon is not perfect; he often makes silly human errors or assumptions, but is easily identified by his concern for others.

II Characters

The most important single element in any human relationship, platonic or otherwise, is love, and Scribe's treatment of it differentiates him from Romantics and Classicists alike. For him, love is neither a passionate infatuation nor a coldly reasoned affection but a deep and abiding emotion. He does not exclude passion, indeed, he sometimes capitalizes on it, but true love can bear the stresses of catastrophe and time. It is not always reasonable, but it is not a dark, raging passion that leads to disaster. It is an intrinsic part of living that promises a good future.

While Scribe creates no genuinely evil characters, he creates no perfect ones either. His people are a realistic mixture of reason and emotion, sense and silliness, practicality and romance, and often a main character is unable to extricate himself from a tangled web. In such cases, a clever friend is necessary, and as long as the cleverness is not directed toward selfish ends, the needs of both comedy and morality are well served.

His female characters are unusual in their strength. Some are physically strong and work their way out of poverty; others are morally strong, standing firm against obstinate fathers or the pressures of friends, and still others are intellectually strong and manipulate circumstances or people with ease. The innocent young ingenue is common in plays with a love chase, but she is usually a minor character, necessary but unimportant. In fact, Scribe appears to have grave reservations about too much simplicity. Some of his least likable characters are frivolous young women with empty minds. Most interesting are those who, faced with serious problems, extricate themselves by their own efforts, or those who create strong opposition for the protagonist.

III Realistic Elements

He also moves away from the practice of the Classic/Romantic schools in his use of theatrical verisimilitude. In part this is achieved by realistic visual trappings, in part by his dialogue. Today it is commonplace to expect realistic language in a realistic play; indeed, in such works, the slightest hint of literary preciosity is a serious flaw, and a dramatist is judged by his skill in making his characters speak in "believable" colloquial terms. To be sure, Romantic theoreticians discussed realism in the theater in terms of "theatrical illusion," but this did not necessarily mean they adopted what we would today call realistic techniques. To contemporary critics, steeped in the tradition of poetic drama with its strictly enforced rules, Scribe's language sounded flat and uninspired. The very elements that worked to his advantage for audiences have been discounted by critics:

Scribe's dialogue is almost entirely composed of brief moments and ellipses. With this abbreviative method, what becomes of the analysis of passion, character painting, the philosophic study of custom, lyricism, style, all the qualities of the poet and thinker? It is good to come to the end according to the precept of Horace, but if it is necessary on the way to throw out one's money, arms, clothing and baggage, what good is the journey[1]

Gautier was apparently unwilling to accept the many levels on which Scribe was working. On the surface, the language is the colloquial speech of the drawing room; the syntax is straightforward, the grammar uncomplicated, the vocabulary neither archaic nor obscure, and there are frequent unfinished sentences and ellipses, with one character finishing another's thought. Such locutions are inadmissible in formal speech, but they have always been accepted in casual conversation, and to have an idea of how cultivated people spoke in the early nineteenth century, one has only to read Scribe's plays. Yet his dialogue is more than a mere reflection of common language patterns; simultaneously it develops the character of the speaker, establishes plotlines and sets the tone. All of this is done so subtly and so adroitly that it seems artless and—to some of his critics—careless. He has, perhaps, succeeded too well in the Horatian art of concealing the artistry.

IV   *Scribe's Concerns*

It would be inaccurate to call Scribe's social comedies satire, for they lack the tragic element necessary to that genre; but it is equally inaccurate to consider them innocuous commentaries on contemporary life. His moral code is too strong to be simplistic; even minor peccadilloes do not pass unscathed. Yet his basic gentleness precludes severe condemnation; the punishment fits the crime, and since the sins are rarely cardinal, justice is tempered.

Courtship and marriage have always been staples of the comic writer, and Scribe is no exception; almost every play is concerned with some aspect of the subject. He adds a new dimension, however, in his emphasis on life after the altar, and his attitude toward marriage is foreshadowed in his attitude toward courtship. His moral values are evident: he shows no frivolous seductions, and adultery is punished severely. Marriage is a serious matter, for it brings responsibility, particularly to men, the sole support of helpless wives and children. Scribe has often been charged with too much interest in financial matters, but in an era without welfare, where poverty literally meant starvation, money was essential. A protected girl, poorly educated and prevented from strenuous activity by custom and costume, would not survive long on her own. Since a proper upbringing did not enable her to make an intelligent choice of husband, this was the obligation of her father, and it then followed that the husband must continue the same kind of protection.

Too much emphasis on such considerations might inject the romantic concept of "all for love" with a certain prosiness, but Scribe avoids this by his concern with other matters. His particular interest is in the relationship itself, the human qualities in a good or bad marriage, and the peripheral questions that affect the individuals involved. Aside from security, a primary focus is compatibility. Similar backgrounds are a distinct advantage, but if the social distance is not too great, either men or women may span them. The partners, however, must have mutual respect for the same basic values; they should also share the same tastes, although the latter is not essential, because they must also accept each other's personal idiosyncrasies. Most important is the moral foundation, for marriage is a permanent state, and Scribe does not regard extramarital affairs lightly. He is not blind to the fact that they exist, but he does not accept them as a way of life.

V   Le Mariage d'Argent

Despite his belief that marriage ought to have a sound fiscal basis, it is clear that he disliked intensely the idea of marriage for money alone, and he makes a distinction between practicality and greed. In *Le Mariage d'argent*,[2] he uses a small group of representative types to illustrate this point.

Dorbeval is a vulgar, materialistic banker; his house, his clothes and his entertainments are lavish, and he is proud of the place he has made for himself. At the opposite extreme is Olivier, a gifted painter who, like all of Scribe's genuine artists, is quiet, industrious and moral. Not the slightest breath of bohemianism touches him, and when Dorbeval suggests an afternoon of amusements, he comments, "You are proposing a stockbroker's day, and I am only an artist . . . I must go to work."[3] Between these two is Poligni, who has elements of each. Poligni, like Olivier, is charming and sensitive, like Dorbeval he is ambitious for wealth, an ambition heightened by his own poverty.

The three women are also individualized, but less by character than by situation. Madame Dorbeval and her old friend, Madame de Brienne, have much in common; both married for money (although for different reasons) and both made the best of their situations. Here the similarity ends, for Madame Dorbeval must live with her decision, and in the end, when it is remarked that she has everything, she replies in a quiet aside, "Except happiness." Madame de Brienne is more honorable and her marriage was a sacrifice. As a young girl she loved Poligni, but her father's bankruptcy put an end to their wedding plans. Brienne offered to pay the debts, but her father could not accept money from anyone outside the family. She therefore married him, even though the sixty-year-old Brienne had not demanded it. Brienne became ambassador to Russia where, after three years he died, and when the play opens, his widow returns to Paris, poor but free, to marry the man she loves. The third woman is Dorbeval's ward, Hermance, a young ninny who thinks of nothing but fashion and balls. She is closely related to the empty materialism of her guardian, but while he is saved from contempt by an honest desire to help others, she is completely selfish.

Given these characters, it is at once apparent that the main action will concern Madame de Brienne and Poligni, and that their marriage will depend upon whether he leans more toward Dorbeval or toward Olivier. The conflict is established when Dorbeval offers Poligni a seat on the Stock Exchange on condition that he marry Hermance and use her dowry to pay for it. Poligni at first rejects the offer and it appears that his principles will prevail, but later when he weakens the conflict develops. In the beginning, his poverty softens his opportunism, but after he meets Madame de Brienne, his choice of money over love forfeits both respect and sympathy.

Scribe increases the pressure by giving Poligni a true choice. After greeting Madame de Brienne warmly enough for her to assume they can marry, he learns that her husband left her nothing, and becomes faced with the options of love in a cottage or an empty marriage in a mansion. The pendulum swings both ways; when Poligni leans toward Hermance, Madame de Brienne inherits a fortune, and for a time it seems he can have both. Unhappily, he chooses too soon. Scribe does not deal in tragic passion, and his characters, although human, seldom cultivate revenge. As a supremely good woman, Madame de Brienne exemplifies the ideal response without compromising her own ethics: she offers her fortune to Poligni in order to save him from the disastrous alliance—but refuses to marry him, knowing his values. It is a fitting punishment, to which Scribe adds a final ironic twist, for Madame de Brienne's offer comes too late; the marriage contract is signed, and Poligni is condemned to the vapid Hermance and the Stock Exchange. She, on the other hand, is rewarded with the faithful Olivier who has long loved her with a devotion she will undoubtedly return.

The most complex character is Poligni, who must have enough good qualities to make his relationship with Madame de Brienne acceptable yet be tainted enough to succumb to temptation. Scribe draws the main lines with exquisite clarity but leaves certain areas ambiguous. Poligni may have been more akin to Olivier when he and Madame de Brienne first loved, changing during her absence when his poverty became unbearable beside Dorbeval's wealth; this would make Madame de Brienne's proffered gift a last effort at reclamation. On the other hand, Madame de Brienne may have fallen in love with his charm and only come to recognize his flaws when she became experienced enough to make a mature judgment; in this case, she has had a narrow escape from Madame Dorbeval's fate.

Madame de Brienne, a simpler character, is some ways more difficult to make believable. She is integrity itself, and her superior character presents problems: if too noble, she becomes priggish, if flawed, she loses her moral strength. Scribe proceeds neatly between the two dangers by giving her unequivocal standards but letting her emotions blind her to certain facts. Thus she may err without either stupidity or moral weakness. She is, without being in the least tragic, a poignant character, for she loses one of the most precious experiences in life, first love. Marriage to Olivier will clearly be much richer and more satisfying than any relationship with Poligni, but it is a mature attachment, and with the loss of Poligni, she also loses her youth. Such poignancy heightens the comedy as implicit commentary subsumes the effervescent humor. Without

didacticism, Scribe presents a case for those values that contribute
to a true marriage. If the audience chooses to ignore the lesson, the
play still provides a delightful evening in the theater; if a thoughtful residue leads to insight, a deeper value is added to the amusement.

VI Rêves d'Amour

Rêves d'amour[4] also touches on the question of true marriage
values, but the emphasis is markedly different. Again Scribe uses
paired characters: the comic focus is on Elise's sentimental illusions,
but the controlling plotline is Jeanne's love story. The two lines are
precisely balanced by the centering of each element in a single
character and the interlocking of their stories.

Elise, the dreamer of the title, is married to Dalibon, who adores
her and hastens to fulfill her every wish. She is unappreciative of his
generosity, for she is wrapped in a cocoon of fantasies that have per-
sisted since her school days when she and her best friend, Amélie,
invented a make-believe future. They promised each other they
would always be together and decided to ensure this blissful state
by Elise's marriage to Amélie's brother. The brother, of course
knew nothing of the plan, but the girls ignored the realities of the
situation and took his participation for granted. Time passed,
Amélie died, and Elise married Dalibon. But when the play opens
she is still morbidly attached to the childish dream.

In contrast is Dalibon's sister, Jeanne, the focus of the marriage
plot and the kind of independent woman Scribe seems to have admired greatly. She refuses to compromise her principles for the sake
of idle dreams and will not marry unless she can find a husband she
can love and respect. Wealthy in her own right, she is not afraid of
the single life:

It is my choice and nothing else. People have strange ideas about what they
call a girl—an old maid. In my mind, it is the most pleasant, most agreeable
life. . . . First, she has none of the household cares; she is not exposed to
the bad humor, the jealousy or the tyranny of a lord and master; she is not
obliged—to keep the peace—to come to terms with the faults of a "better
half." Free and independent, she need not account to anyone for her actions, her thoughts or her secrets—if she has any![5]

The two women are linked by a situation which has become so
critical that the slightest pressure can bring disaster. Elise's

marriage is in trouble, for as she retreats from reality, she abandons her marital responsibilities; already Jeanne has taken over the entire management of the household. Jeanne too has reached a crucial point; uncomfortably close to being an old maid, in spite of her brave words, her future promises little. These lines are tied together in the person of Henri, who is not only the ideal partner for Jeanne, but also the long-since-vanished brother of Amélie. His presence, which alone is enough to convince Elise that he has come for her, produces enough complications to make his real purpose of proposing to Jeanne a secondary matter until the climax.

The plot is light, and the comic opportunities for intrigue are plentiful, but it is not simple farce. As long as Elise continues her present self-deception, her future is in serious jeopardy, for her husband cannot compete with a dream lover. The imaginary Henri has grown in stature over the years, but once the real one appears, she must choose between him and her husband. Jeanne, on the other hand, must change her allegiance from a brother to a husband, leaving behind falsely sterile independence for a union that promises both life and a true valuation of her person.

As always, Scribe's message, though not spelled out, is inherent in every scene and character. It is not a statement against romanticism—certainly Henri, who has gone adventuring and made his fortune is a romantic figure—but rather a clear demonstration of the difficulties stemming from false illusions. He is creating comedy, not teaching a lesson, but both humor and dramatic impact are intensified by the linked contrasts.

VII   La Famille Riquebourg

La Famille Riquebourg, ou le Mariage mal assorti[6] takes up another kind of relationship, and the true state of the marriage gives an ironic twist to the title. Monsieur Riquebourg is even more gauche than Dorbeval; a self-made man, he has become a rich merchant by honest industry, without having ever lost the accent and manners of the Marseillais clerk he once was. His wealth has brought him position and a countess as a wife, but his crudeness has made him a laughingstock among her friends. Like Dalibon, he genuinely loves and admires his wife; on her part, Hortense, although forced to marry him (by her family), not only respects him but has come to regard him as "my dearest friend, my guide, my protector," and by her behavior has brought others to respect him.

The title plays on the idea of a seeming versus a real misalliance, but within the family a real mismatching has developed in a love between Hortense and Georges, Riquebourg's nephew. Since no honorable resolution is possible and continued propinquity is both painful and dangerous, one of them must leave. Without giving her husband the full explanation that would surely hurt him, Hortense offers to go to the country; but when Georges understands her reasons, he accepts the responsibility and himself departs.

The climax of this play is a fine example of Scribe's ability to knit all elements into a unified entity and to underscore the theme without direct statement. In the first scene, Riquebourg is counting out funds with which to send Dampier, his cashier, off to Havana. Dampier is a carefully developed offstage character, a young married man who is reluctant to leave his family in France, but who, to retain his position, must. In the last scene he is taking a tearful leave below in the courtyard when Georges resolves both his own problem and Dampier's by offering to go to Havana himself. Riquebourg had wanted Georges to stay in Paris and marry Hortense's niece, Elise, but by this scene it is clear that Elise loves someone else. With one speech, Scribe ties together four plot lines, as Georges says, "Tell him [Dampier] to stay. I shall take his place."[7] The continued stability of the Riquebourg ménage is assured, the incipient affair of Georges and Hortense broken off, Elise's marriage made possible and the Dampier question answered. The preparation is so subtle that the surprise is not dissipated, and it is so logical that it does not appear contrived.

The rupture of the Georges/Hortense affair is visibly painful to them, for they are passionately attached; but it lessens in importance when weighed beside the inevitable guilt that would follow the breakdown of the Riquebourgs' marriage. Passion, Scribe seems to be saying, can be sweet and true, but its values are not to be compared with those of a permanent relationship.

VIII   Dix Ans de la Vie d'Une Femme

Not all women are as honorable as Hortense Riquebourg, and when one is vicious, she must pay a high price. She is Adèle in *Dix Ans de la vie d'une femme*, who relinquishes a perfectly good marriage to pass from lover to lover in a gradually descending scale until she reaches the lowest level and death. It is a serious thesis with no room for comedy, whose severe morality appears outmoded in the twentieth century; nevertheless, the scenes are dramatically effective, and the characters ring true even today.

IX   Oscar

Scribe holds the same standards for both sexes in terms of extramarital alliances, and any guilty party will be punished. Yet he is aware of social practices, and his plays reveal a double standard of treatment. If a woman falls, it is serious, but errant men are ridiculed. In *Oscar, ou le Mari qui trompe sa femme*,[8] he pokes fun at the philandering male. Oscar is fundamentally a "good" character, for he genuinely loves his wife, but he has deceived her because, he says:

Every evening we stayed home together, and since one cannot always talk, we read. . . . I became acquainted with the new literature that has dethroned the old . . . with its storms of the heart, criminal and delirious passions . . . its heroes of the modern drama who, after having trampled all social restraints underfoot, blow out their brains at the climax. All that, except the climax, gave me infinite pleasure. From reading about such things, I began to dream about them, and from dreaming, I aspired to commit them.[9]

His punishment is as severe as farce will allow, but the message is clear. Oscar suffers not only from fear that his wife will discover his lapse, but from a sense of guilt as well.

In comic fashion, he gives himself away by his treatment of his wife. She, like any clever Scribean woman, quickly recognizes that unusual deference to her wishes and unexpected gifts are certain symptoms that he has a mistress, knowledge which she immediately turns to her advantage. She too is a "good" character, for she uses her power to assist the young notary, Thérigny, in his desire to marry her cousin.

There are complex pairings in this work, for the two male Bonnivets, Oscar and his uncle Gédéon, are pitted against Juliette Bonnivet and the maid Manette, but each pair is a contrast in itself. Gédéon is an old *roué*, sophisticated, clever and devious—but also selfish, living only for his own pleasure. He will claim ownership of a suspicious ribbon to save Oscar, but is also quite aware that to do so enhances his own raffish reputation. Oscar is a mere shadow of his uncle, a would-be rake, unsuccessful at the mildest deception;

but he, at least, does not pride himself on his exploits, and has the grace of shame.

In the contest of wits, the women are clearly the winners, for each is successful in her own way. Juliette outmaneuvers both men on every count and is a mistress of intrigue. Manette is a mere tool, but even in her awkward attempts at blackmail, is more adept than either of the men, and gains the one thing she wants—marriage to Chanteloup, her offstage sweetheart.

The plot is complicated, but Scribe keeps the audience fully aware of the developments at all times, while keeping the characters from knowing too much before the climax (a difficult task accomplished by his parcelling out information piecemeal and through the use of subplots). Juliette offers to assist Thérigny, certain she will succeed because of her husband's guilty conscience; Oscar confirms this by informing his uncle of his assignation with an unknown woman. These two lines cross and countercross as Oscar tries to keep Juliette from knowing, and Juliette presses her advantage, using Manette to threaten revelation by saying, "I know all." Manette knows of neither line, but she complies for her own purposes. As Oscar becomes more deeply enmeshed, he becomes accordingly more ridiculous until, with what should be his ultimate humiliation, Juliette reveals she herself was the woman he met.

With a true satirist, the play would be a savage commentary on unfaithfulness, but because Scribe stays in the realm of comedy, the laughter elicited is lighthearted. Husband and wife are well matched; their love is true and the future is optimistic for them and for Manette—who has faithfully waited for her Chanteloup. Only the rake, Gédéon, is left alone at the end, but even he is not punished severely, and only his pride is injured.

X   Une Chaîne

The question of marital fidelity is again treated in *Une chaîne*.[10] The unifying thread is the love story of Emmeric and Aline, but the body of the play concerns the obstacle of Emmeric's past affair with Louise, married to one of his best friends. Aline's guardian will not give permission for their marriage until he has written assurance that Emmeric is free. Since such a document will necessarily compromise the woman, the difficulty seems insurmountable.

Here Scribe pairs Emmeric and his closest friend, Hector, with a novel twist. Emmeric has placed himself in a predicament from which Hector releases him—but involuntarily and with unexpected consequences—for he is no *raisonneur*. It is Emmeric who suggests that the eminently respectable Hector has had the affair; this protects himself and, instead of reflecting adversely on Hector, has just the opposite effect, giving him precisely the romantic dash he had lacked and leading to his own marriage.

The character of Louise in this play is particularly unusual, for in the eyes of the audience, she has forfeited all respect. Even Scribe's enemies, Dumas fils and Emile Augier, subscribed to the dictum that "once a woman has fallen, she may never rise again."[11] Scribe presents her sympathetically and even offers redemption. Because her husband, Vice-Admiral Saint-Gérans, had neglected her shamefully, it was quite natural for her to turn to the embraces of the ardent young Emmeric. She is not promiscuous, however, for there is no doubt that she loved the young man and continues to do so. Once she learns that for him the affair is over and that he genuinely loves Aline, she performs the greatest sacrifice possible: she writes the letter freeing him and signs her name. The action is final; she will not take another lover, and Scribe pardons her fully. Her signature is never seen, the letter is burned onstage, and the admiral realizes that his neglect could permanently damage their marriage, although he never learns of the affair.

Scribe neither condones infidelity nor does he accept it as an answer to the arranged marriage. Yet he is not unaware that ex-tramarital liaisons, temporary or permanent, are part of his society. Ideally, his marriage partners hold their vows sacred, and many of his plays exemplify his standards. His humaneness, however, keeps him from being unduly harsh, even to the traditionally unforgivable woman.

Although part of his gentle treatment may derive from the necessity to maintain the comic tone, he clearly has strong feelings on the subject. If unfaithful men are ridiculous, unfaithful women are either vicious or victims. Adèle in *Dix Ans de la vie d'une femme* is an example of viciousness and is destroyed; Louise has been misguided by circumstances and so escapes punishment.

XI   La Chanoinesse

A similar unfortunate woman is treated in *La Chanoinesse*,[12] in which the heroine has a son, the result of a rape seven years previously. She has since led an exemplary life in retirement, caring for the child that she says belongs to her niece, and is finally rewarded when the guilty father, delighted to marry her and to recognize his son, returns, an almost unheard of conclusion for the day, but consistent with Scribe's moral stance.

XII Feu Lionel

In *Feu Lionel*[13] he attacks the same materialistic element of society as in *Le Mariage d'argent,* but with such a different treatment and focus that the two plays have little in common except the money question itself. In treatment, *Feu Lionel* approaches pure farce, but it remains in the realm of social comedy because of its underlying theme. The focus is less on marriage (although that is part of the plot) than on the consequences of equating social status with finances. Scribe's position on money is perhaps most clearly illustrated in this work.

He uses extremes to show his point; references to death are as frequent as the hilarity. Wealthy young Lionel went to Paris and became attached to a group of much richer people whose values were based on money. He was soon out of his depth and out of cash, entangled with the Baroness who headed the group. Having staked all on one last gamble which he lost, he knew he had also lost the Baroness, because in her world such a loss made him "shameful, worse—ridiculous!"[14]

Unable to face ridicule and poverty, Lionel determined to end it all, wrote farewell notes to all his friends and threw himself in the river. Even his suicide was a failure, for he was netted by a fisherman, hauled out with the daily catch and sent on his way. Shortly after, he happened to be at a railroad station just in time to rescue old Brémontier from an onrushing train. In the course of the rescue, he sprained his ankle, and Brémontier's grateful daughter, Alice, invited him to stay with them during his recuperation.

All of this has happened before the curtain rises, allowing Lionel and Alice time to fall in love. But the present situation is given immediate stress when Brémontier complains to Alice that Rigaud (the name Lionel has taken) has outstayed his welcome and will soon have to leave. Although love has altered Lionel's materialistic Parisian values, even in the provinces he cannot live without some income, and the love affair begins to look gloomy.

The satire, keener than in most of Scribe's work, is also in a different form. Lionel is a ridiculous figure not only because of his foolish behavior, but because he is also terrified of being considered so by others; and the resolution of the play depends upon turning ridicule from one target to another. Pairing Lionel with Brémontier's clerk—the sagacious Montgiron—allows Scribe to show the contrast between Lionel's values and Montgiron's shrewd common sense while resolving the problem, for Montgiron is, at last, a full-fledged *raisonneur*.

If there is any real change in the later plays, aside from length, it is in Scribe's treatment of plot complications. In developing situations he began to rely more and more on the single character of the *raisonneur*. Here Montgiron's cleverness and capability are responsible not only for the satisfactory *dénouement*, but when set against Lionel's bumbling and confusion, heighten the tension of the conflict. Montigron is admirable, for all his skill is at the service of others, and any distrustful overtones raised by his extreme intellectual facility are obviated by his motives and his success.

The main plot cannot be resolved without external assistance, for Brémontier is adamant and the young couple helpless. The prospect of such help arrives when it is discovered that Lionel's only relative has left him a fortune and the neighboring estate. This is manifestly too slight for a full-length play, and Scribe's complexities not only fill out the body of the action, but serve to heighten both the satire and the characterizations. To do this, he brings in the Parisian element, the Baroness and her new admirer, Robertin, setting their values against those of Alice and Montgiron. The excuse for their appearance is plausible—the Baroness wants to buy the neighboring estate. The effect is multiple: Lionel is forced to make a choice, the plot complications increase and the comic opportunities are amplified.

Scribe shows no mercy to the Baroness and Robertin. Within her circle, she is extremely successful, for she is greedy, clever and unscrupulous. She can sense a money making scheme, can outsmart most businessmen and has no hesitation in trading on her feminine charm. Robertin is her current favorite because, despite his insensitivity, dullness and coarse manners, he is wealthy. Each of them complements the other in a grotesque parody of the love between Lionel and Alice.

The climax comes when Lionel is forced to make the impossible choice: should he reveal himself or not? If he does not, he will lose the estate and Alice; if he does, he will gain his estate, but will be subjected to public scorn and probably lose Alice anyway. The dilemma is highly comic, but the moral question is serious; and when Lionel elects to bear the scorn and trust himself to Alice's love, he redeems all his past foolishness. The climax is inevitable, but the reward is unexpected and typically Scribean in its deceptive simplicity: Montgiron asks Lionel to pay off a fictitious bet; supposedly he had wagered that if Lionel were to disappear for six months, the Baroness would forget him—which she has. In an instant the laughter is turned against those who deserve it most.

While Scribe is never didactic, the moral stance is clear and, in fact, is part of the pleasure. It is not simply a matter of rewarding right and punishing wrong; the resolution lies in Lionel's choice. The terms may be trivial, but the values are still being questioned a century later.

XIII   La Fille de Trente Ans

In *La Fille de trente ans,*[15] Scribe satirizes false social values connected with courtship and marriage. The values of a good marriage have been discussed elsewhere, but for the purposes of this play it is, perhaps, important to repeat that once the marriage contract was signed, each partner was irrevocably tied to the other, whatever the future might bring.

He approaches the question obliquely, first introducing Lamorinière, the rich old bachelor who has vowed never to marry but to devote himself to pleasure. Past fifty, he has nearly ruined his nephew, Robert, now following closely in his uncle's path. Lamorinière is admittedly corrupt in his pursuit of Ursule, the "girl" of the title:

I wish her no evil—on the contrary! But, proud and ambitious, she has placed her virtue on an elevated pedestal that can be seen from afar but not attained. One day, like my sister Anne, she will no longer have worshippers—then, angry and despised, she will descend, like so many others, from the pedestal. For a clever man who knows how to profit by the occasion . . .[16]

Robert is not actually paired with his uncle but with his old school friend, Raoul, who has Montgiron's values without his cleverness. Robert, the manipulator, actually standing in Lionel's moral position at the opening can go either toward his uncle's or toward Raoul's values. Since he is not the protagonist, his conver-

sion comes quite early; in the second act he is assailed by a castoff
mistress and arrested for debt. The stay in prison evidently brings
him to a more serious view of life, for after Raoul rescues him, he
goes to work and begins to consider a new road, "I don't speak of a
fortune—that's not important; But a gentle, sweet companion, a
lovely character—that will last forever!"[17]

The women are also paired but function on different levels. They
reveal a sharp contrast in values: Ursule is manipulative, self-
serving and false; her actions govern all others. Hélène is gentle,
self-sacrificing and true; there is no need for her to undergo a conversion parallel to Robert's because she, like Raoul, is consistent
throughout.

Even more clearly than in *Feu Lionel*, plot intrigue is embodied
in character, and the conflict develops through two manipulators
pitted against each other. Ursule is the more complex; as the
daughter of a Vice-Admiral, her dowry is not large, but she has excellent social standing. Nevertheless, she has repeatedly refused all
proposals of marriage, and at thirty years of age still regards herself
as a young girl. She is furious when a salesgirl addresses her as
"madame," and chides her father for not accompanying her to the
shops. Her unmarried status is beginning to worry her, and
Lamorinière's description is unflattering:

With her ambitious pretensions, she demanded nothing less than a title
with an immense fortune! Today she should be less difficult. By insisting on
her choice, she sees her aims diminish, and as the throngs of suitors disappear, she can scarcely hide her resentment, and while she is still charming and affectionate, under the soft words . . . one can feel the sharp edge
of the old maid—outraged at being single, jealous of others' happiness, pale
at the sight of her friend's wedding dress.[18]

His assessment is correct, and her panic is evident in an incident
with the Marquis de Villiers. Although the marquis is a dolt, she
had built his reputation as a means of making him propose to
her—only to discover that when her efforts had made him attractive
enough for his cousin to marry—Ursule was left an unwilling
recipient of his gratitude. The disappointment should engender
sympathy, for Ursule is already in a bad position. She had once
refused Raoul, but now sees her error and wants to marry him; it is
obvious, however, that Hélène and Raoul are in love, prevented
from acting upon their desires only because she is rich and he is not.
Despite the fact that Ursule knows their feelings, she proceeds with

her scheme to catch Raoul, telling each that the other loves someone else and dispelling all sympathy for her misfortunes.

Her plan is complicated by other characters; Hélène is affianced to Robert, but the crisis of his debts breaks off the match, while his arrest brings Raoul back from London to rescue him. Meanwhile, Lamorinière contributes a further development by writing a note suggesting that Ursule become his mistress; he does not intend to send it until the appropriate moment; but when it accidentally falls into her father's hands, a duel threatens.

Robert, aware of Ursule's tricks and determined to thwart her, provides the solution to both plot lines by assuring Lamorinière that the only way to avoid the duel is to make Ursule an honorable proposal. The idea is anathema to both, but Lamorinière has no alternative, and neither does Ursule after Raoul and Hélène reveal their love to each other. She had previously toyed with the idea of marrying Lamorinière for his wealth, imagining herself a rich widow within a few years. She is almost pacified until Scribe adds a final elegant touch to her punishment: Lamorinière admits that in place of an income of sixty thousand francs a year, he receives only forty-eight thousand in an annuity that will cease with his death.

The comedy is amusing, but the ridicule is obvious and, for Scribe, severe. It will be as painful for Lamorinière to adjust to the married state as it will be for Ursule to have to hope he lives a long time. Scribe finds neither the old *roué* nor the professional virgin pleasing; both prey on others, both corrupt society, and neither accepts the responsibilities of life.

XIV   Le Camaraderie

La Camaraderie[19] uses a love story as the basis for a satire on the coteries that build and maintain reputations in the artistic and political worlds. The love story, however, is merely the unifying factor, and it is at times completely obscured by the intrigues and richly comic characters of the satiric portions. The moral lines are cleanly drawn. On the side of the angels are Edmond, a young lawyer, Agathe, the girl he loves, and Zoë, Agathe's closest friend. Opposed to them are Césarine, her cousin Oscar, and a clique of self-serving frauds. In the center, Agathe's father, the Count de Miremont, serves as a balancewheel that can grant victory to either side.

The brilliant, ambitious young Edmond loves, and is loved by

Agathe; but they cannot marry because he has to make his way professionally. His prospects improve when a place as deputy becomes available; he is obviously the right choice, but he must be confirmed by an election and, without the backing of votes, has little chance to succeed. With the deputy's position as a focus, the forces on each side are lined up. Agathe and Zoë help Edmond, Césarine and her clique form the enemy. The two younger women are typically paired characters with the same values, but as a well-bred, unmarried girl, Agathe can do little, while Zoë is a rudimentary *raisonneur*. Agathe's love assumes deeper significance when viewed in conjunction with Zoë's unhappy marriage, and the audience's sympathies are engaged by the juxtaposition.

They are also paired in their struggle against Césarine, their former schoolmistress, now Agathe's stepmother. Césarine, who deliberately married for wealth and position, contrasts sharply with the pair and is the most corrupt character in the play, for she is motivated exclusively by selfishness and a lust for power. She is not, however, pure evil, because Scribe has assigned perfectly logical, if reprehensible, reasons for her actions. An intelligent girl, born into the lower classes, she took advantage of every opportunity and married into the upper class. Her husband's position has allowed her to build a circle of sycophants, until at last she has arrived at the point where she can exercise real power. Her methods have been devious and her ends serve only her immediate needs; even when she behaves admirably, her motives are meretricious—she is a perfect wife only because she wants her husband's influence.

Her marriage, loveless by choice, begins to show stress when Edmond appears. Césarine once loved him but chose wealth and power; now that she is secure, she realizes what she has missed and wants him back. Possibly she has a dim recognition of true worth, for in spite of the false world she has chosen, she is his intellectual equal and in other circumstances might have made him a perfect wife.

She has made her choice, however, and it is irrevocable. Scribe may admire her potential, but he deplores her actions, and does not spare the sycophantic clique. Among them are a poet, a painter, a doctor, a librarian, each claiming to be the best of his kind. Scribe has great fun in the scenes where each admires the others' ridiculously bad achievements. The most important for Césarine's purposes are Dr. Bernardet, who gathers votes when she promises him a government position, and Zoë's husband, Montlucar, who owns a newspaper and puts the power of the press at her disposal. The special focus of Césarine's efforts is her cousin, Oscar, a vain, stupid, self-proclaimed genius, who embodies all the worst elements of the clique. Césarine decides to make him a deputy, and with her powerful assistance, there is no doubt he will become one of France's lawmakers.

If Scribe is not gentle in satirizing the clique, he is very much so in his portrait of the Count de Miremont. It is difficult to avoid making an older man with a young wife look like a fool, particularly when she is quite willing to betray him. Scribe resolves the difficulty by making Miremont the only means of securing Agathe's happiness. In terms of comedy he is important, for he is the only bulwark against the negative power of the clique, and until Edmond is elected, is also the only "good" character in government. It is a delicate balance, achieved by presenting him as an affectionate father and respected statesman, and by keeping him aloof from the machinations of the clique. This eliminates contempt, but Scribe does more: it is clear that his first marriage was happy, that his wife's death left him a lonely widower and that, accustomed to honesty in personal relations, he did not recognize Césarine's wiles for what they were. He feels a genuine love for her, and Césarine's manipulation of that love not only gains sympathy for Miremont but removes it from her.

Scribe also develops his theme with plot reversal. In the beginning, Césarine wants the deputy's post for Oscar until, with some hints from Zoë, she believes Edmond loves her. Ignoring her cousin's feelings, she at once offers to assist Edmond, who because his sense of honor forbids him to use personal connections for professional advancement, refuses her. Meanwhile Zoë prevents both Edmond and Césarine from learning the truth until the last moment. When Césarine learns that Edmond actually loves Agathe, she tries to change the votes, but it is too late; she loses the election and with it some of her power.

As always, Scribe works upon several levels simultaneously; Edmond's integrity is essential to establish the moral basis of the love story, but the fact that it does not permit him to accept devious methods to attain his desire allows for considerable plot complication. Both Zoë and Césarine must help him in spite of himself, while the possibility of his discovering their maneuvers adds suspense and reversal to the story. The marriage question is also on several levels, for it involves not only a matter of immediate happiness but the future. If Edmond does not gain the appointment, his alternatives are dreary: he can find another group to support him or he can remain in his present near starvation position. His moral standards will not allow the first, and remaining in place dooms any idea of marriage. Agathe's prospect is even worse, for it is clear she will soon be forced into a marriage at least as unhappy as Zoë's. An unfortunate end to the courtship, then, will continue the corruption of Césarine's clique, suggest the collapse of integrity and deprive not only the individuals but France itself of hope. The surface is a polished love comedy that moves rapidly with one highly amusing scene after another; but beneath the laughter is a serious foundation, and the implication that the political, social and artistic governance of France is primarily in the hands of fools is not at all humorous. The implication is indirect, but it engages the unconscious emotions as the rapid activity captures the conscious attention. The combination assures both present pleasure and a lasting reflection.

XV   Les Doigts de Fée

Les Doigts de fée[20] is a late work which reveals, perhaps more than any other, Scribe's concern for characterization. But it is noteworthy for other reasons as well. There is less of the usual intrigue, and the emphasis on changing social conditions is clearly stressed. Most strikingly, the two strongest characters are women, the Dowager Countess de Lesneven and her granddaughter, Hélène.

The Count de Lesneven heads the cadet branch of an aristocratic Breton family; Hélène is the last representative of the older branch, but, because of Salic law, cannot inherit her father's dukedom and lives as a poor relation in the Count's home, barely tolerated and treated as little more than a servant. The fundamental conflict is between the Count's mother, the Dowager Countess, and Hélène, for they represent two opposing elements of midnineteenth-century society. The Dowager exemplifies the old Breton aristocracy, perhaps the last remaining vestige of prerevolutionary days, when lineage determined social position, and noblemen were above ordinary life. Hélène is the new nobility, the blood line still intact but not above honorable labor and achieving a position by means of it. In the early scenes, the Dowager has all the power, but in the end, it is evident that Scribe's sympathies are with Hélène.

Each woman is paired with a man, and in each case, she is the stronger. The Count is not only weaker than his mother, he is meaner, for he complains bitterly about the cost of supporting Hélène. His carping is unjustified, since she is inordinately grateful for every favor and spends all her time catering to the family's whims. In the younger pair, Hélène is distinctly stronger than the Count's son, Tristan, and Scribe shows the disparity very early. When Tristan announces in Act I that he wishes to be a lawyer, the Dowager will not hear of a Lesneven working. Tristan reluctantly but definitely bows to her will.

Tristan and Hélène love each other, but the Dowager wants him to marry a rich heiress, preferably Berthe, another cousin, in spite of the fact that Berthe does not love him. Berthe admires Hélène, and, although the latter outshines her in every way, the only rivalry between them is in the minds of the Count and the Dowager. At first, the Dowager succeeds, for Hélène, aware of the family's wishes, refuses Tristan's proposal of marriage. Even so, the proposal arouses such sharp hostility from the Dowager and the Count that Hélène is forced to leave and make her way alone.

An ordinary woman in such circumstances would be expected to turn to the streets, but Hélène is no Adèle (*Dix Ans de la vie d'une femme*). She has one remarkable gift; it is established early that she is a superb seamstress and utilizes this talent to support herself. Two years later she is literally the most powerful woman in France, for she creates gowns for the wives of governmental leaders. Whatever she wants, these women are eager to give, and they do not hesitate to pressure their husbands if her wish concerns public policy. She now has the strength necessary to face the Dowager, and the climax displays the sharp differences between the corrupt old regime and its selfish abuse of power, with the new one and its generous, proper application. In the last act, Tristan, discouraged by losing both the opportunity for a career and the woman he loves, has squandered his fortune and is deeply in debt. The Count cannot help him, because he has invested all his available funds in land, hoping that the government is planning to build a railroad through it; he too is on the brink of ruin when it becomes evident that the railway may go in another direction. Hélène uses her influence to put the railroad through the Count's land and then, with supreme generosity, gives Tristan the money she had saved to pay the last of the mortgage on her shop.

Such a gesture deserves reward and, of course, Hélène and

Tristan are allowed to marry, but the treatment of the *dénouement* is not only unusual but displays Scribe's concern for his characterization. In the performed version, the Dowager is so overwhelmed by Hélène's gift that she withdraws her opposition to the marriage. This was consistent with plot expectations but not with the character as Scribe had drawn it, and he remarked:

We would suppose, according to the rules established by masters of the art, that the Countess, consistent to the end in her Breton prejudices and pride, would not give in unless constrained by force. The public judged otherwise, and they are always right . . .[21]

His original scene gave the Dowager no sudden change of heart; in that version she had accepted Hélène's largesse but was even more adamant against the marriage because of Hélène's entrance into trade. Scribe acceded to the critics' complaints, but when he published the play, he took a mild revenge, printing both;

It was censured, and we changed it in the theatre to obey the critics; we put it back in here to satisfy our literary conscience . . . The public will judge and provincial directors may choose between the two versions.[22]

Scribe's point had been that only power can bend the Dowager's will, and Tristan exerts power by threatening that if she continues to refuse her blessing to his marriage with Hélène:

I myself will be the accountant, the book-keeper, the cashier . . . and proud of our state, I shall make it known throughout all Paris—from tomorrow, on our escutcheon—yes, grandmother, that is what they call the signboard—an escutcheon. Our coat of arms on a field of gold with "Hélène, Duchess of Lesneven, Couturière.[23]

The prospect of Tristan sitting behind a cash register is too much for the old Dowager and she gasps her compliance; it remains only for the Count, who obeys his mother in all things, to give his official approval. Scribe is clearly concerned with the building of manyfaceted characters, particularly in the later plays. He does not probe and develop in detail, but sketches in all the necessary lines and leaves it for actors to fill in the substance.

XVI   Bataille de Dames

Bataille de Dames[24] was written in 1851, when the political tribulations of 1815 - 1818 had faded into history. But Scribe uses the troubled year of 1817 for an action that might have occurred at any time. One of his most popular comedies, it has been translated and frequently played in English.[25] The title is actually a pun, for the "battle" is twofold: one part concerns the struggle between two women for Henri's love, the other sets the women against the government as personified by Montrichard. The two plots complement and reinforce each other, while the shifting of emphasis never allows the attention of the audience to waver.

The action concerns Henri de Flavigneul, a young Bonapartist now wanted as a traitor by the monarchy. He is not, in fact, a traitor, but because he has been sentenced to death, is hiding in the Countess' home, disguised as a servant, until he can cross the nearby border and escape permanently. The love plot has developed as a result of his extended stay in the Countess' home; the intrigue begins when Baron Montrichard appears on a mission to apprehend him.

The Countess, the central figure in both plots, is a rare woman who draws sympathy and admiration. As a wealthy widow, she is an independent person who could be an ideal wife, but who is also strong enough to stand alone. She is beautiful, intelligent, witty and honorable, but more important, all her gifts are at the service of her friends and family. Montrichard is a formidable opponent with undeniable brilliance and adept at intrigue; the Countess increases in stature when she is able to defeat him.

This is not simply a play of intrigue, however. The struggle between the women ends in the Countess' defeat, adding a poignant twist to her victory over Montrichard. The situation of an older and a younger woman in conflict over a man is fairly common in drama, but the struggle between the Countess and her niece, Léonie, is unusual. Neither woman is a predator, and it is obvious that either would give up Henri's love for the sake of the other. To the audience, the Countess is clearly the superior, for in the battle with Montrichard, Léonie repeatedly loses the advantage won by her aunt. Less beautiful and less gifted, Léonie does have one overwhelming advantage—she is the right age for Henri. Scribe never matches older women with young men and, although Henri is

clearly attracted to the Countess and only a few years separate
them, marriage is impossible and any other relationship un-
thinkable. On the other hand, because the love between Henri and
Léonie is natural and true, the audience can accept the inevitable,
and the comedy is deepened by the bittersweet perception.

XVII   *The Characteristics of the Social Plays*

Scribe's sense of humor may lead him to find men ridiculous, but
he never becomes contemptuous. He may show their values to be
false, but his understanding and acceptance of their motives
prevents a satiric emphasis on negative aspects. Though such an attitude, essential for comedy, can lead to superficiality and contrived
endings, he is seldom guilty of such gaucherie. Indeed, the variety
of his plots is so extensive that he rarely repeats himself, and each
play seems a unique idea. The conclusion may be inevitable but
there is no way to foretell how he will reach it.

He usually defines characters by situation, but also incorporates
an old tradition in the process. The use of paired characters reaches
back as far as the valiant Roland and the wise Olivier, where the
qualities of each character emerge by contrast. Working within that
tradition, his inventive touch not only led to the use of that useful
creation, the *raisonneur*, but demonstrated as well an economical
way to develop plot, provide variety and clarify thematic material
simultaneously. It was a valuable lesson for later playwrights.

His plays set in contemporary times are commonly called "social
comedies," but perhaps a more accurate term would be "moral
comedies." He is less a social reformer than one seriously concerned
with the moral problems of his ever changing society. His political
sympathies are clearly republican, but he is not blind to the flaws he
sees in a world which ostensibly has repudiated the old aristocratic
values while hypocritically still paying them secret homage. The
corruption of political, social and artistic standards which distresses
him, he deals with only by implication. His particular interest, and
indeed the continued charm of his work, lies in how the individual
behaves when faced with a specific problem.

Marriage plays a large part in these works, and quite naturally so,
since it was a principle preoccupation of his audiences. Yet to consider him as merely a writer of romantic comedies following simple
formulas, is manifestly unfair. He is concerned with the general
welfare, but he does not let external matters, fleeting or lasting, in-

terfere with his primary function of creating a play that will interest and amuse in the theater. The range of Scribe's interests is remarkable, and if he consistently uses a love story as his connecting thread, he enlarges it far beyond its ordinarily restricted area. Scribe has much to say, and says it superlatively well in a way that not only was palatable to his own audience but is clearly valid today.

CHAPTER 4

The History Plays

I *The Nature of Historical Drama*

IN the creation of any historical drama, two basic problems are immediate: theatrical need and accuracy. Circumstances rarely conform to the needs of the stage; geographically and temporally they are strewn across a wide area, and the multiplicity of detail is too florid for the limitations of the playwright's art. If he includes everything, the work loses focus, if he oversimplifies, it loses force. In terms of accuracy, the writer of fantasy, satire or propaganda is allowed some flexibility, but one who attempts verisimilitude is locked into a series of events of which the audience has prior knowledge. His historical personages have certain well-defined and accepted attributes that must conform to the commonly received image, or else the work as a whole forfeits its validity.

With such difficulties facing an author whose work must be concluded in less than three hours, it might be wondered why any playwright would choose to become a chronicler when invented stories offer so much more freedom to the imagination. Yet, despite the obvious problems, history is a rich source, offering a variegated tapestry of strong characters, powerful emotions and earthshaking confrontations. Properly utilized, the known outcome of a single moment can add weight to the drama itself, giving an external importance to the internal relationships and deeds.

It has been charged that Scribe had no interest in history, but it would be more accurate to say that he simply did not write dramatized history. Clearly fascinated by the past, his interest is not limited to his own country; all Europe provided a canvas for Scribe's plays, while his operas and vaudevilles are often set in the Near or Far East. His "foreign" characters assume no special distinction; they may have slightly different customs and laws, but

86

their souls reside in regulation human bodies motivated by recognizable needs and desires. His heroes not only have feet of clay, they are made entirely of clay—human clay. Leaders, he says, are no different from other men except by way of their positions. They have eyes and weep, they fall in love, and they are subject to quite ordinary ills and passions.

Scribe does not denigrate historic accomplishment, he merely doubts that it was achieved by purely grand means. Although he does not lose sight of serious matters, his approach is primarily comic. Usually a love affair functions as the connecting thread of the plot, its successful conclusion affecting graver matters, just as a stone dropped into a pond creates ever widening ripples. Here is a distinctly modern, nonheroic and personalized view of the past in which nobility may be part of an unconscious cultural heritage—but behavior is triggered by immediate psychological and emotional needs.

Scribe is generally apolitical as far as specific party affiliation is concerned, but a survey of these works indicates strong republican loyalties. He is not a blind idealist; he sees the faults of a society which has replaced respect for high birth with respect for great wealth. Yet he remains a fervent believer in a structure that offers hope to those willing to work. More than any other single form of government or society, he fears and loathes absolute power; to him it represents the destruction of all decent human relationships. Power is not intrinsically evil but a fact of society. Scribe is not against the fact, but recognizes the temptation presented by it, and understands human beings well enough to realize their weaknesses. The greater the power, the greater the temptation, he concludes, not far apart from Lord Acton's "absolute power corrupts absolutely." Nevertheless, it is clear that in any given group some will be stronger than others, and Scribe bases his moral evaluations on how they use that strength. The danger of despotism is dehumanization, and if one succumbs to the temptation of absolutism and disregards human values, the result is negative. He may retain material possessions but lose all others. For him who uses it to serve others, the result is positive. Such a person gains love, acceptance and the sympathy of the audience.

The tight structure of the well-made play may seem inimical to the presentation of anything that might justifiably be called "history," but for Scribe it is an advantage. The narrow limits prevent too broad a sweep of incident and force out all events and characters extraneous to the main dramatic line. To the historian, interested in the tapestry of the past, such simplification is tantamount to omitting half the stitches in the picture; but to the audience in the theater, the very simplicity permits an intense view of one corner, with the same advantage Sidney claimed for the poet:

the historian . . . is so tied, not to what should be but to what is, to the particular truth of things and not to the general reason of things, that his example draweth no necessary consequence, and therefore a less fruitful doctrine. . . . the peerless poet . . . giveth a perfect picture of it by some one by whom he presupposeth it was done; so as he coupleth the general notion with the particular example.[1]

By placing immutable historical facts on the periphery and focusing his main attention on a fictional behind-the-scenes action, Scribe can observe all known facts scrupulously without losing the freedom to invent characters and relationships. The approach is well within tradition, for it is, in a sense, what the epic poet does, and it has long been a favorite mode of French writers.[2] The use of a fictional main plot allows the writer to manipulate history by offering alternate explanations for documented facts, but while Scribe's choice of alternatives produced amusing comedies, they also brought him into direct conflict with sentimentalists who preferred marble statues to living beings.

II Thibault

His approach is manifest as early as *Thibault, Comte de Champagne*,[3] a slight one-act *comédie-vaudeville* based on the thirteenth-century aristocrat-poet who became king of Navarre. The subject is light and the treatment fanciful, in keeping with this type of drama, but the external framework is fairly true. There was an actual Thibault, and an incident much like the one in the play could well have occurred. Without altering the frame, Scribe has created an independent action whose controlling line is a love story, while the historical context provides echoes of grandeur absent from a more contemporary setting.

The real Thibault was married to Blanche de Castille, but his wife in the play is Marie de Bretagne, whose brother has initiated a war by murdering Thibault's followers on the wedding night. Thibault managed to escape and raise an army against the Duke de Bretagne, but his belief that Marie must have been privy to the plot has led him to distrust all women. During a lull in the hostilities, Marie appears with Thibault's oldest friend whom she had saved at the risk of her own life; she is exonerated, and the play ends with a reconciliation. The license taken would obviously outrage historians, yet the factual germ of the story cannot be denied, and it is an attractive presentation of Thibault's character.

III   Avant, Pendant et Après

A more serious view is in the three-act comedy, *Avant, pendant et après*.[4] This is not, strictly speaking, an historical play with known figures from the past, but is instead a fictionalized action based upon recognizable events. It is, perhaps, as close as Scribe ever came to writing a thesis play demonstrating his views on the past fifty years in France, along with his moral judgment of those who lived them.

Actually, it is not a single play but three one-acts, linked by a set of characters seen under varied circumstances. The main lines are established in the *"Avant"* section, in which the class distinctions are clearly drawn. The year is 1787, and the aristocracy rules. The Duchess de Surgy has educated her two sons to continue the system; the elder, the Marquis, accepts and enjoys his privileged status, but the younger Chevalier displays a rudimentary social conscience and is consequently at odds with his mother. The catalyst for the action is a young orphan, Julie, ward of the Duchess, who has grown up in the family. Both young men want her, but the Marquis is merely lustful, while the Chevalier loves and wants to marry her. The Duchess simplifies matters by coldbloodedly convincing Julie that her low station obliges her to marry Gerard, a rather dull young farmer. Her plan is executed by her henchman, Goberville, and the true lovers are painfully but effectively separated, for both are too honorable to break the marriage sacrament.

In *"Pendant,"* which takes place during the Terror, the grotesqueries of the revolutionaries are not spared. People have taken new names, having servants is forbidden, and ridiculous new laws are made every day. The marriage of Julie and Gerard is solid; he is a good man who adores her, and even without love, she respects him.

Their existence in these unsettled days is precarious, especially when the proscribed Marquis takes refuge in their house. He is being hunted by Goberville, now a power in the revolutionary government, and is saved only by the Chevalier, who has become a general in the army, but who openly disapproves of the Terror, "Ah, do not confuse liberty with the excesses committed in its name. Liberty, as we understand it, is the friend of order and duty, it protects rights. It approves laws and institutions, not scaffolds."[5] His is the voice of reason, the voice of Scribe passing judgment on the madness of the past.

The "*Après*" segment takes place in 1828. Of the three kinds of societies, this is the only one that offers hope for a better future. In the holocaust and what followed, much good was destroyed, but much evil as well. Gerard died at Wagram, but the Duchess and the Marquis are also dead, and with them the injustice of the old aristocracy. The Chevalier has married Julie and they have a daughter he hopes to marry to his nephew, the Marquis's son. An old friend, the Vicomte de Morlière, turns up after having been marooned on a desert island for forty years, and much of the commentary on the changes in French life are supplied by this relic from the past. He is horrified to learn that everyone, even a peer, is taxed, must pay his debts or go to prison, and is expected to work for a living.

The most profound changes are evident in the young people and in the hope they offer. Goberville returns as an influential journalist contending with the Chevalier for a deputy's seat. He too has a nephew, Derneval, who, although lacking the background and breeding of the Marquis's son, has nonetheless become a promising young attorney and is in love with the Chevalier's daughter. Such presumption would not have been tolerated in the old days, the Vicomte remarks, but the Chevalier recognizes that Derneval is worthy of the girl. The ancient enmity between the classes is ended, and the Chevalier states the promise of a new age:

Let me not punish the children for the sins of their father; merit and honor, wherever they are found, have the right to our esteem.[6]

Goberville will not forgive, but it does not matter, for he has become an anachronism as surely as the Vicomte. In the new age, reason, ethics and justice prevail.

IV   Salvoisy

A somewhat different view of preRevolutionary France is given in the two-act comedy, *Salvoisy, ou l'Amoureux de la reine.*[7] On the surface, it appears more sympathetic, for Marie Antoinette is neither corrupt nor vicious. She is, however, a stranger to the passionate depths of emotion that is part of Salvoisy's character, and her capacity for love is not indicated until after the Revolution is underway and she is fleeing for her life.

The connecting love story stands in sharp contrast to an unfeeling court atmosphere. Louise, a poor orphan brought up by Salvoisy's mother, has made a long and difficult journey from Epargny to the Trianon because she loves Salvoisy and is concerned for his welfare. He, himself, it is soon discovered, was a member of a revolutionary group dedicated to the assassination of the royal family, who while on a reconnaissance mission, saw and fell in love with the queen. Since that time he has followed her everywhere, lurking in gardens and palace rooms whenever he can slip past the guards. Louise identifies him, and he is brought face to face with Marie Antoinette; but the queen, not recognizing his love for what it is, orders him remanded to the custody of his mother. In view of his past activities, he is fortunate not to be sent to the Bastille, but the shock of being coldly received by his idol is too much, and he goes mad.

The second act takes place four years later. Salvoisy is still insane, tended by the faithful Louise whom he imagines to be the queen. At this point, Scribe takes some liberty with known history, for Marie Antoinette and an ailing Dauphin arrive at Epargny, closely pursued by her enemies. According to the records, the royal family traveled together in their vain attempt to escape, but this liberty serves the dramatic purpose when the sight of the queen shocks Salvoisy back into his senses. The plot turns rapidly from this moment on; the queen is overtaken by her pursuers who do not recognize her, the now sane Salvoisy continues to feign madness and saves her.

The last scenes of the play not only demonstrate Scribe's facility for complication and clarification, but also serve as an example of the many levels on which he simultaneously operates. The love theme evident in Louise's steadfast devotion is finally resolved when Salvoisy, returned to normalcy, realizes he loves her. During the same process, however, other kinds of love and their values are

being worked out: the queen, so concerned with trivial matters in
the first scene, displays genuine maternal tenderness under the
stress of adversity; the pursuing captain who cares for no one, con-
temptuously humors Salvoisy when the latter asks for a safe con-
duct, and his contempt is turned against himself when the safe con-
duct permits Marie Antoinette to escape; Salvoisy, as his true self,
has deep sympathy for the unfortunate mother, and, rejecting his
revolutionary ties along with his madness, repays the crown that
once spared his life.

The *dénouement* is shot through with irony. It is clear that
Salvoisy can only obtain his love through a return to sanity, yet
rationality cannot function when the society is mad, and the comedy balances delicately between the two states in a treatment unusual for a time when madness was usually the basis for melodrama.
The other irony, connected to the observer's knowledge of the past,
is more typical of Scribe; so much sympathy has been generated for
the queen that the audience is eager to see her evade the clutches of
the captain, and much of the tension is built about this point. It is
resolved successfully, but no matter how cleverly the difficulties are
overcome, the facts of history are inexorable; Marie Antoinette will
end her life on the guillotine, and the comedic conclusion is colored
by the awareness of her future.

V   Le Moulin de Javelle

A more lighthearted but nonetheless incisive view of the moral
turpitude is seen in *Le Moulin de Javelle*,[8] a two-act *comédie-
vaudeville* set during the Regency of 1718. It was rather a daring
subject, for the leading character is Philippe, Duc d'Orléans, grandfather of Louis-Philippe, who was occupying the French throne
when the play was first performed. Orléans had been Regent during
the minority of Louis XV and was known as one of the most
profligate aristocrats in French history, along with his closest ad-
visor and companion, the Abbé Dubois, financial genius and later
cardinal. They are opposed by the ambitious Duchess du Maine.
The characters are straight from the pages of history, as is the web
of events peripheral to the central action. Scribe uses real details to
knit together his fictionalized story. The Duchess' coconspirator is a
Spaniard, and their plot against the Regent's life is a logical precur-
sor to the war with Spain that began in 1719.

The aristocrats are all morally reprehensible, their power and position used for self-gratification. The Regent's attention is almost entirely centered on his efforts to gain Babet, a young working girl, as his mistress; Dubois maintains a bevy of beauties, and the Duchess wishes to overturn the government by force. Scribe is not so much against aristocracy as against any system that operates independently of the human spirit; in this play, the aristocracy becomes a metaphor for such a system.

The central question is one of love, and each of the three main characters must learn its meaning. In the beginning, Babet takes the false hierarchy of birth seriously; she had run away from home because she loved d'Aubigny but considered his social position too far above hers for marriage. She agrees to marry "M. François" (the Regent masquerading as a clerk) because she thinks he is of her class, not realizing he has no intention of marrying her. Only when she learns his true identity and purpose does she allow her true feelings to overrule the false values. D'Aubigny's lesson is political; having been misguided by the Duchess into an assassination plot against the Regent, he is saved from the negative consequences by his love for Babet, which deflects his murderous plans.

These two characters serve to bind fact and fiction, but the theme is personified by the Regent himself. Early in the play, as he states his dishonorable intentions toward Babet and remarks that her innocence had attracted him, the Abbé warns him, "Take care, love is a strange thing that cannot be commanded."[9] The Regent laughs off the warning, but he learns a lesson. Both plotlines, the love story and the power struggle, reach a climax at the same time; the Regent wins the battle for power but at the cost of revealing his true identity. When Babet learns who he is, she refuses to have anything more to do with him, and he realizes that he has indeed fallen in love with her. Her attempted suicide at this point convinces him he has lost her forever; he relinquishes her to d'Aubigny, satisfying the demands of the comedy, but leaving a bittersweet residue to the conclusion.

If this were solely a political statement, it might be expected that the lower classes would be pure and unselfish, but Scribe is not writing a polemic. Babet's friends among the working class are perfectly willing to be corrupted by the Abbé and "M. François." Only Babet and d'Aubigny, representing both upper and lower classes, are untainted, set apart by their honesty and their love for each other. Though it is not a history lesson, the humanity of the characters offers a perception that cannot be achieved by a cold recital of facts.

VI   Adrienne Lecouvreur

The background of *Adrienne Lecouvreur*,[10] Scribe's one tragedy based on historical incident, has been discussed earlier, but the treatment is different enough from his usual approach to warrant a closer examination. The subject was well chosen; it seemed ideal for the greatest tragic acress of the nineteenth century to play the greatest tragic actress of the eighteenth, and it required relatively little adaptation to flesh it out into a five-act play. Perhaps because the story itself is so dramatic, Scribe did not waver from a known history, choosing real people for his main characters and adding fictional characters only to provide motivation and contrast for the central action.

Although the story of Adrienne Lecouvreur is well documented, the events at the conclusion of her life are shrouded in mystery. Even here, however, some facts are well known. She did give forty thousand francs to her lover, Maurice de Saxe, for an expedition to regain his duchy; the expedition was a failure, and Maurice returned to Paris a year later minus both duchy and funds. The romantic escapade made him the darling of the aristocratic ladies, and, while he maintained his liaison with Lecouvreur, it seems he was also enjoying the favors of several others, prominent among whom was the Duchess de Bouillon. The Duchess, determined to remove a dangerous rival, asked the Abbé de Chazeuil to procure some poison for her, which he did; but then, overcome by remorse, the Abbé confessed to the authorities who at once set a police guard around the actress.

Saxe seems to have been singularly dull about women, for the next recorded incident shows him at the Théâtre Français in the Duchess' box, during a performance of *Phèdre*, when Lecouvreur was playing the title role. In the eighteenth century, both house and stage remained lighted during performance, so that it would have been almost impossible for Lecouvreur not to notice the Duchess and Saxe together. She angrily threw the famous lines of Phèdre toward the Duchess' box in a public insult enjoyed by a knowledgeable audience. The Duchess, refusing to lose face, invited Lecouvreur to her box and publicly presented her with a bouquet which had been impregnated with poison. Four days later, Lecouvreur was dead.

A modern scholar might wonder if the poison story were true, for the Duchess' guilt is only circumstantial. Lecouvreur had been ill for months, and the autopsy disclosed no indication of poison; only the situation and the sudden death of the actress were the bases for the malicious speculation that followed.[11]

Scribe takes the outline of the story and develops it into a five-act tragedy, resolving the multiple problems with ease. Four problems, in particular, are worth noting. The first is the problem of the poison which is only on the edge of believability. He sets the first act in the boudoir of the Duchess (whom he has elevated to Princess), makes her husband a dilettante scientist interested in poisons, and introduces a box of unknown substance that the Prince has been asked to analyze. The effects of the poison are known and described, then set aside without further reference. But the seed has been planted, and Scribe has the information to use when needed.[12]

A second difficulty is the scene in which Lecouvreur insults the Duchess, since it takes place both on the stage and in the audience. Scribe removes it from the theater completely and sets it in the Princess' home, where Lecouvreur has been invited to give a reading. This serves several purposes: it vastly simplifies the staging of a play within a play, and at the same time makes Lecouvreur's insult more deliberate and impressive to the onlookers.

A third, and perhaps equally difficult problem is that of the Princess' character. Scribe does not write incarnate evil; although he has a very clear delineation of corruption, his characters remain well within the bounds of humanity. The aristocrats here are corrupt; Scribe gives the Prince an affair with another actress at the theater, according the Princess a strong reason for her own unfaithfulness. It may not be commendable, but it is understandable. This affair is also used to show the Princess' cleverness, for she has enlisted the Prince's inamorata as a spy. The single complication not only builds the Princess' character but satisfies the unspoken question: why should a woman with power, beauty, position and intellect feel the need to poison her rival?

The bouquet is a fourth problem. In characteristic fashion, Scribe weaves it into the plot well in advance of the time he needs it. In the very first act, Maurice appears with a small nosegay in his lapel that he claims to have bought from a flower girl. The Princess, convinced it was given to him by another woman, pretends it was meant for her and takes it, revealing both her jealousy and her perception. In the last act, the same bouquet is returned to Adrienne, who thinks it is from Maurice, breaking their relationship. Grief stricken, she clasps it, inhaling its deadly fragrance, and when Maurice appears to declare his love, it is already too late. Adrienne, in a hallucinatory frenzy from the poison, dies in his arms.

One of the main difficulties of this kind of play is to prevent it from becoming pure melodrama, for the events are not of themselves inevitable. Scribe knits the highly colored events together by means of a series of logical situations, so that the outcome is the only possible one. It is not a tragedy of character, but Adrienne is a poignant figure, and her death is tragically ironic. Implicit in a tragic actress' actual death is the question of theatrical and external reality, while the vision of an actress playing an actress compounds the difficulties presented by the question. The delicacy with which Scribe blends the two realities into a single creation may explain why the piece long remained a favorite with actresses and audiences not only in France but across Europe and in the United States as well.

Cilea's opera *Adriana Lecouvreur* (1902), which has remained a stage favorite, gives testimony to the emotional impact of the plot, in spite of the fact that Cilea's librettists, in adapting Scribe's play, were required by the needs of opera, to sacrifice some of the important details of motivation and dramatic necessity which are at the heart of the dramatic action.

VII   *Two Russian Plays*

Scribe's history plays are not restricted to France. He was evidently intrigued with Russia; two plays are set in that country which reveal a kind of double vision: neither the essential human qualities nor Scribe's attitude toward power are changed by geography, but he occasionally takes a rather parochial attitude toward other cultures.

Chut![13] is a two-act *comédie-vaudeville* set in the eighteenth century court of Catherine II, and, as always, the historical frame is accurate. He has, however, allowed himself considerable freedom in the invention of a fictional plot that will fit the known boundaries. The main love plot is the kind of backstage incident that might have occurred. The characters are essentially no different from parallel characters in the French plays, but they also have certain traits Scribe evidently considered particularly Russian: a volatile people with sudden and exaggerated displays of emotion, unpredictable reactions and a touch of barbaric cruelty. They are nonetheless likable, even admirable, and while Scribe finds their bizarre actions amusing, he shows neither contempt nor pity for their lack of Gallicism.

Two major historical figures are used. Catherine II, czarina of Russia, remains offstage but has a powerful influence on the action, while her lover, Prince Potemkin, plays a leading role. Scribe, who was attracted by the extravagant and romantic figure of Potemkin has the niece exclaim:

> I admire you, Potemkin, how your character unites the best and the worst at the same time! Completely the Russian empire of which you are the bulwark, and living image, you are, like it [the empire] half civilized, half barbarian. In you is mingled the Asiatic, the European, the Tartar and the Cossack![14]

The moral distinctions are clear. As in all centers of absolute power, the court of Catherine the Great is corrupt, with the licentious Czarina at the nadir of the moral scale. Her lover, Potemkin, is the onstage personification of immorality—but all the courtiers are touched with it. Only Ladislas, the young Polish army officer, is exempt. An extraordinary combination of naivete and audacity, he has fallen in love with Potemkin's niece, the Countess Braniska, given up his military career and appears in St. Petersburg solely to be near the Countess. Potemkin is violently possessive of his niece, and without Catherine's protection, Ladislas's life would undoubtedly come to a swift end. In the new favorite, Potemkin sees the end of his power, but he cannot have Ladislas executed without incurring the Czarina's wrath. Faced with the typically Scribean impossible choice, he can resolve it only by bringing about a marriage between the Countess and Ladislas.

The intrigue is as complex as it is amusing. Through most of the play, Ladislas confides all his hopes and plans either to "Grigorief" (Potemkin in disguise) or to his cousin Alexina, who is working for Potemkin's downfall. Each of these plots against the other but is constantly foiled by Ladislas's ignorance of court politics and the royal favor he enjoys. His ignorance keeps him innocent, until in the end he is rewarded with a fortune, an estate in the Ukraine and the woman he loves. Yet, from the courtiers' standpoint, his success is not complete; Potemkin has had a narrow escape but remains the favorite, and the others understand the opportunity Ladislas has lost. The irony of the situation is delightful comedy, underscoring

humanistic values even as it points to their material disadvantages.
Russian atmosphere is also the setting for *Un trait de Paul I$_{er}$, ou
le Czar et la vivandière,*[15] a one-act dealing with Catherine's son
who succeeded her in 1796. Here the exaggeration is particularly
stressed in the character of the Czar who is not only exceedingly
volatile, but has the power to enforce his whims.[16] He has a morbid
fear of assassination, and indeed, was assassinated in 1801; his comments about his parents can be verified by any biography, and factual details are carefully built into the fiction. At the very end, as
the main characters are about to be sent to Siberia, an offstage
Napoleon functions as a *deus ex machina:* referring to Paul's disastrous Italian campaign against Napoleon, Scribe incorporates a
message from the French general announcing that he is returning
one thousand captive Russian soldiers "newly dressed and armed."
To surpass this noble gesture, Paul releases the lovers, endows them
generously and sends them off to France. With a single stroke,
Scribe has served the comic necessity, poked gentle fun at the
Russians and paid a gracious compliment to his own country.

VIII   Bertrand et Raton

When the scene shifts to Denmark, the characters are less exotic;
his Danes are, in fact, French in the way that Shakespeare's Italians
are English. The violence inherent in his Russian characters is absent in Danish people; but in *Bertrand et Raton, ou l'Art de con-
spirer*[17] it appears in the crowd that forms an audible background
through most of the play. The corruption of the court is less gently
treated than it is in works with a French setting; the aristocratic antagonists are not at all sympathetic, and the lower classes are more
sharply satirized. The story concerns the fall of Struensee, the German doctor who became virtual dictator of Denmark. The time
period can be precisely dated, January 16 - 17, 1772. Within this
framework, Scribe has created a complex network of plots and
counterplots as the characters vie for the power of the throne.
Struensee came to the Danish court in 1768, as personal physician
to Christian VII, who had fallen ill during a tour of his kingdom.
Circumstances proved favorable for a meteoric rise: Christian was a
weak ruler dominated by a mother and a wife at odds with each
other. Struensee, strong, intelligent and physically attractive, soon
occupied a position similar to that Rasputin was to occupy in the
Russian court; in three years he was the most powerful man in the

country and began a series of reforms that shook the foundations of Danish society. Between March 1771 and January 1772, he signed over a thousand orders aimed at altering the status of serfs, reorganizing the municipal governments and changing the legal system. The old aristocracy, headed by the Queen-mother, strongly opposed all reforms and set about removing him from power. On January 17, they struck; Struensee and the Queen were arrested, and shortly after, he admitted to being her lover. She was incarcerated privately, he was executed.

Neither Struensee nor the Queen appears onstage, but the forces on each side are clearly drawn. Representing those in power are Count de Falkenskield and Goelher, both ambitious and corrupt. The Count is a member of Struensee's council and so eager to rise that he is willing to sacrifice his daughter's happiness; Goelher covets Bertrand's position as minister, although his sole qualification is a talent for dancing. Their most visible antagonist is Julie-Marie, the equally corrupt Queen-mother who wants to regain power through her royal son and whose motto is "the end justifies the means."[18]

Between the two camps and dominating the action stands one of the most interesting characters Scribe ever created. Bertrand de Rantzau begins as a neutral in the struggle for power and ends as the true ruler of Denmark. His most outstanding trait is his principled rationality; against it are set the ambition, greed and ignorance of the others. Bertrand, who opposes unbridled power that seizes authority without regard for legitimacy, refuses to use his political talents simply for the sake of reward. Both are admirable traits, but it is his intelligence and cleverness that place him in the unusual position of leading character and *raisonneur*.

His actions are based on a deep concern for human values. In typical Scribean manner, the great event of Struensee's fall is occasioned by the small cause of two young lovers, Eric Burkenstaff and Christine de Falkenskield. Bertrand, unmoved by Julie-Marie's plea for assistance in overthrowing Struensee, is touched when he learns that Christine's father has dismissed Eric and is forcing her to marry Goelher. His sympathy initiates the machinations that eventually bring down the existing power structure.

The love story is a trigger, but the target is power, and the question involves political morality when it becomes evident that Struensee wants the throne for himself. Scribe does not preach divine right, but he clearly believes in a lawful and peaceful succession nonetheless. Given a choice between a weak but legitimate ruler and a dictator bent on power for its own sake, Scribe opts for natural order—with the precaution of placing a wise counselor beside the king.

Bertrand's method demonstrates his rationality, in its precise orchestration of human motivations. His chief tools are Raton Burkenstaff, a self-important and ignorant bourgeois who represents the unreliable populace, and Colonel Koller, whose overwhelming desire to be named general leads him to betray his own men. Bertrand knows how to touch certain sensitive nerves, and without ever seeming to make a decisive move until the last critical moment, he plays on a range of emotions that destroy his enemies and elevate his friends.

While the structure is essentially comic, Scribe maintains a nice balance of tragi-satiric overtones. Raton's vaunted love of the people suffers a severe setback when their demonstration on his behalf leads them to smash his shopwindows and steal his goods. His extravagant libertarianism becomes ridiculous when set against the pragmatism of his wife. Both are inferior to Bertrand who blends idealism with reason to win the day.

Scribe keeps the melodramatic events of history off the stage, focusing the action on Bertrand's varied intrigues as unified by the love story. The result is a sense of intensely vivified history coupled with a moral judgment reinforcing Scribe's basic tenet that concern for human dignity must subsume all viable political structures. Julie-Marie may gain the regency, but it is Bertrand who will make Denmark strong.

IX Maître Jean

Political implications are not always the major concern in the history plays. *Maître Jean, ou la Comédie à la cour,*[19] a two-act *comédie-vaudeville*, has a background of political intrigue, but the primary focus is on a question that would fascinate playwrights at the end of the century, the question of the reality/unreality principle in theatrical representation. Scribe, of course, does not approach it from the standpoint of a Pirandello, but if the treatment is vastly different, the fundamental question is nonetheless the same.

The scene is Weimar, at the court of Duke Karl Augustus; the year is 1775, when young Johann Wolfgang von Goethe was the duke's guest. The raffish "Prince" (his title in the play) is encouraged in his follies by the Duchess de Stadion, who is conspiring to gain control of Saxe-Weimar. To the court comes Goethe's grandfather, an old peasant deeply suspicious of the theater and anxious to protect his relative from its evil influences. His peasant's simplicity and goodness, however, prevent him from interpreting events correctly, and the conflict between the real and the unreal stems from this point. Jean's initial suspicions are converted to enthusiastic loyalty when he overhears the Prince reading a speech from Goethe's play and believes it reflects the royal sentiments. Soon disabused, he stubbornly retains his good opinion of the Prince, in which he is shown justified at the end.

Once he "understands" play-acting, Jean is determined not to be hoodwinked again—at which point Scribe reverses the positions. Jean watches what he believes to be a rehearsal but is actually the Duchess and her fellow conspirators. When he reports to the court at large on the "scene" the intrigue is revealed, the Prince agrees to marry and settle down, and Goethe is established as the court poet. While political-moral statements are incorporated into the whole picture, Scribe's focus is on drama as a kind of reality. Jean's response builds the comedy, but the question is philosophical, and in the midst of laughter there still lingers an uneasy sense of another dimension yet to be investigated.

X Contes de la Reine de Navarre

Contes de la reine de Navarre, ou la Revanche de Pavie[20] moves the scene to Spain. Set in the sixteenth century, it is earlier than most of Scribe's historical plays, but in treatment and theme it relates closely to *Bataille de dames*. It is essentially a comedy of intrigue in which the women are pitted against the men in a battle that never leaves the palace. The weapon is wit, because, as Marguerite says, "I am a woman! To protect and save all that I love, I have only the weapons heaven has given me: deceit and skill."[21] The resolution is her clear victory in the eyes of the audience, and an equally clear victory for Charles V in the eyes of the other characters.

Scribe took as his subject the efforts of Marguerite to free her brother, François I, from his imprisonment by Charles V after the battle of Pavia. He has telescoped the five years from Pavia (1525) to the marriage of François and Eleanor of Austria (1530) into a few days, but he has managed to include most of the ramifications that evolved from these circumstances. He has taken the barest facts only, giving himself enough flexibility to create an amusing alternative explanation for history.

The primary struggle is between Charles V, Emperor of Austria, and Marguerite, the French princess who became Queen of Navarre. One of Scribe's strongest heroines, Marguerite is decidedly superior to all the other characters. Charles is extremely clever, ruthless, powerful and proud, but in these very qualities lie the seeds of his eventual destruction, for despite his admiration for Marguerite's political judgment, he ignores her sound advice and insists on going his own way. Scribe is not explicit, but relies on the knowledge that history will record his eventual downfall. François is weak but charming, with a quixotic sense of honor that overrides common sense. He refuses to attempt escape disguised as a monk for fear that discovery would make him appear ridiculous; on the other hand, he also refuses to give Charles Burgundy because that would despoil France. He is by turns petty and grand, a romantic hero whose real strength comes from his sister.

Marguerite stands in strong contrast to the emptyheaded Infanta Isabella who will eventually marry Charles, and to the unhappy Eleanor, dominated by her brother, Charles. Eleanor secretly loves François, and their marriage is entirely the work of Marguerite, who, by diplomatically allowing Charles to take the credit, seals the peace of Madrid, the fall of Spain and her own lovematch with the King of Navarre.

Part of the humor lies in the balancing of minor characters in the complex love affairs that proceed in conjunction with the political intrigue. The ambitious Guattinara has an ongoing affair with Babiéça's wife, Sanchette. She, in turn, adores Henri d'Albert, in love with Marguerite. Charles is also dazzled by Marguerite, although he is engaged to Isabella, who loves Guattinara. Political and love plots intertwine, but the masterful construction never allows them to thicken beyond comprehension.

The play has nationalistic overtones. François's determination to abdicate in favor of his son, thus keeping the titular rule of France out of Charles's hands, is a moment· guaranteed to tighten the throats of patriotic Frenchmen. Yet Scribe never loses control of the comedy, and, indeed, some of his own philosophy may be visible in the grudging tribute Charles pays his brilliant antagonist, Marguerite, "I know nothing more difficult to vanquish than wisdom that laughs."[22] In the end, the grace of laughter conquers all.

XI   La Bohémienne

Another play that does not deal directly with the power question is *La Bohémienne, ou l'Amérique en 1775*[23] which takes place in Boston on the eve of the revolution. It is less "historic" than most of these works; if peripheral events and characters are in line with known facts, the primary story is pure romantic fiction. The situation is a Scribe favorite: two antagonists with a catalyst between, providing the conflict with a unifying thread that allows maximum imaginative freedom.

The action takes place during the last days of Lord Gage's rule as governor of Boston, when the tension was approaching the climax of Bunker Hill. Scribe's sympathies are with the Americans, but Gage is shown as an honorable man who loves his daughter Henriette[24] and who honestly tries to administer justice. The Americans, led by Lionel Lincoln are waiting for French assistance to arrive before beginning their offensive. They meet and plan their moves at an inn where, it happens, a Bohemian gypsy and his niece are staying. The gypsy, Zamparo, is searching for his brother, and his story becomes involved with the burgeoning revolution, for he has been a professional spy, and his presence in Boston is viewed with deep suspicion both by Gage, who knows him, and by the Americans who think he is a British sympathizer. Thickening the intrigue are the love stories of Henriette and Arthur Winkerton, captain of the Virginia dragoons, and of Bathilde and Lionel. The first involves the question of liberty, the second unites all the various intrigues.

The structure is comedic, and in the end the Americans have taken their first successful steps toward independence, Henriette and Arthur are united, and Gage, his life saved by Lionel, is off to England. The last circumstance is crucial, for it is closely interwoven with the story of Bathilde, who is not only the most sympathetic character, but is the only one whose reward is questionable. As an infant, she was stolen by gypsies and is revealed finally as Gage's long-lost daughter he had believed dead.[25] Having been reared away from cities and courts, she is the "purest" and most innocent of all, and under ordinary circumstances her future might be assured. Her innocence, however, is a result of ignorance and in the end, feeling unworthy of Lionel, she gives him up to return to England with her father and learn how to become a lady. Nothing in her behavior indicates more than a lack of social grace, surely not essential in revolutionary America, but her choice gives Gage some compensation for Henriette's allegiance to the Americans and avoids too heavy a penalty on an upright man who happened to be born on the wrong side. Since Bathilde freely chooses to go with her father, the conclusion is poignant rather than painful.

Scribe obviously admires the Americans and takes their cause seriously, but he does not permit his sympathies to interfere with his comic purpose. He frequently breaks the dramatic tension by introducing a satiric element, as when the English fop, Sir Cokney, bemoans the lack of tea in Boston. He pits the naive but honest new world against the sophisticated and corrupt old Europe and honesty wins. Nevertheless, he is not romantic about the victory, and both sides have their ridiculous moments.

XII   Fils de Cromwell

He was clearly fond of the eighteenth century, and most of the history plays are set within this time. He was also particularly drawn toward England, and no fewer than five plays are concerned with that country's past. The pattern is the same, but the emphasis on the corruption of the court is perhaps more overtly developed than in any other nationality. In *Fils de Cromwell, ou une Restauration*[26] the restoration of Charles II forms the background for the central question, the effect of absolute power on the individual. Scribe favors neither Cavalier nor Puritan, but depicts both as corrupt power seekers and sets them against the honesty of Richard Cromwell, son of the Protector.

As the play opens, Oliver has been dead for two years, and the government of England has become a shambles. Charles has been asked to mount the throne but is opposed by the Cromwellians who want to keep the power for themselves. Richard, who has been living in Berkshire under an assumed name, is the natural leader of the Puritans, but his sojourn in the country has reinforced a value system alien to that of the power bloc. At one point he is persuaded that duty commands him back to Whitehall, but when the greed and ambition that surround him there preclude any honest human relationship, he resigns.

Richard, who turns his back on power, is the only man worthy of it, and in Scribe's view neither king nor Puritan is fit to rule. Charles, a thoroughly reprehensible character unconcerned for the welfare of his people, uses his royal prerogatives solely for selfish pleasures. He propositions all women, even Lady Terringham, who shelters him from Puritan troops, he sees London as a gigantic pleasure palace, and offers neither gratitude nor reward to the faithful servitors whose efforts have returned him to the throne. On the other hand, Ephraim Kilseen and General Lambert, the chief Puritans are, if possible, even less concerned with the general good. Their downfall is a matter of record; but despite the recognition of Richard's principles and the satisfactory conclusion to his love story, the play ends ironically. If the tone is not exactly despairing, it is nonetheless bleak, and the prognosis for Stuart England is not optimistic.

XIII La Favorite

Unabashed corruption in a royal court forms the basis for *La Favorite*,[27] a one-act *comédie-vaudeville* set in the time of James II. History here is only a vague excuse for this comedy of intrigue, but the underlying motif of corruption is inescapable. Scribe has taken considerable liberty with dates, and, for him, the references are mark .dly inaccurate.

Lord Sunderland, out of favor since the death of Charles II, plots with a Puritan neighbor to kidnap Arabella Churchill, mistress of James and their enemy. Sunderland arranges for his nephew Arthur to carry her off, hoping that the resultant scandal will destroy her credit with the king and raise theirs; but the Puritan's niece is captured instead. Of course, Arthur and the niece are already in love and, after some mistaken identity crises, are united. Sunderland's ignoble ambitions for power, the Puritan's greed for his niece's fortune are foiled, and only the innocent young couple are rewarded with happiness. An oblique irony suggests that the hatred displayed by the Sunderland group will fester—as it did—and in the near future explode. The romantic conclusion to the love story contrasts sharply with the reality of James's rapidly approaching fall.

XIV Le Verre d'Eau

Le Verre d'eau,[29] the most famous of the history plays, is also concerned with intrigue. The factual background is exact, although

Scribe has condensed the time element, juxtaposing Abigail Masham's entry into the court (1706), the fall of Marlborough (1709) and the Treaty of Utrecht (1713). The time is approximately 1712, the place St. James's Palace, and the sovereign, Queen Anne. She is unlike Scribe's other rulers in that she is moral, although not particularly admirable and lacking the vision of a great ruler. Nevertheless, she occupies the seat of power. The conflict between the formidable Duchess of Marlborough and Bolingbroke is for the control of that same power.

The Duchess and Bolingbroke are beautifully balanced opposites. Each is an expert at court intrigue, each is a daring gambler for power, and each is confident of success. Here the parallel ends, for the moral division is clearcut; the Duchess is concerned only with herself, Bolingbroke cares for others. The Duchess is perfectly willing to have the war continue; it keeps the Whigs in power and her husband on the continent, leaving her free to amuse herself with Arthur Masham,[30] a handsome young officer she has arranged to have at court. To this end, she manipulates the Queen with lies, false compliments and veiled threats, forfeiting royal affection for the strength of fear. Bolingbroke is easily the Duchess' equal in manipulating people and events, but his purposes are unselfish; he wants peace for the country, he has genuine sympathy for the Queen, and he spares no effort to aid the two young lovers, Abigail and Arthur. In the end, he must be the victor.

The portrait of Queen Anne is, according to history, accurate; she and Sarah Churchill had been close friends since girlhood, but they were at loggerheads in their later years, and the Duchess' violent temper outbursts finally drove them asunder. The rupture was foreseen by some Tory leaders, who introduced Abigail into Anne's court to hasten it. Anne was evidently slow to break the friendship, and Scribe gives her a strong reason; as a childless widow, her only hope of keeping the Stuarts on the throne is a Parliamentary bill allowing her half-brother, the son of James II, to inherit the crown. The Duchess' promise to effect this succession gives her the needed hold over Anne until other considerations supervene.

These considerations form the connecting thread of the action, which focuses on young Masham, beloved of Abigail, the Duchess and the Queen. The successful outcome of his love for Abigail is the foundation for the comedy, and the unrequited loves of the two noble ladies provide the elements for intrigue. Together, all three lines form a clear example of moral forces in conflict. The ideal love of youth is favored by Bolingbroke who represents the party of peace; the Duchess, representing the war party, has only lascivious desire. The seat of power, the Queen, vacillates between the two and, in the end, finds victory in defeat. She loses her hope for love but she wins peace for her country.

The subtitle, "Cause and Effect" is a statement of the theme that great events arise from small causes. In this case, the end of the war, the fall of Marlborough, the victory of the Tories and the successful outcome of a love affair derive from the single instance of a spilled glass of water. Despite this lighthearted approach, Scribe stays fairly close to history and the outcome coincides with known facts.

It is, however, the moral question that holds Scribe's attention. Except for the young lovers, all main characters are tainted by the power they hold. The Duchess is the most obvious, since she uses hers for personal gratification at the expense of those about her; but even the Queen is not exempt. As a victim, Anne is sympathetic. But it is clear that her state decisions are based on private considerations, not on principle, and while those decisions lead to a happy conclusion, they are the product of Bolingbroke's carefully engineered pressures, not of her own independent thought. Bolingbroke's charm and wit make him attractive, but his motives are questionable. Playing court politics with skill and grace wins the game without much concern for morality on his part, and it is almost by chance that the good of England is served. The weight of known history gives scope to the comedy, but the satiric edge gives it a rare depth, and it has remained a favorite with audiences.[31]

XV   Sir Hugues

Scribe's view of the English court may have been tempered by French republicanism, for without exception he presents it as a center of corruption. In *Sir Hugues de Guilfort*,[32] George I is shown as a dissolute womanizer who does not hesitate to proposition the most helpless lady in his court and who scarcely bothers to conceal his affairs from his Queen. Scribe does not moralize, but has considerable fun at the monarch's expense, as when Sir Hugues indicates that the Queen has a love tryst, then prevents George from leaving the room to stop it. The unexpected reversal of a rake into betrayed husband is a novel one, and if the moral question is temporarily muddled, it is soon clarified; meanwhile the comic effect is considerable.

XVI   L'Ambitieux

One of Scribe's most famous plays is *l'Ambitieux*,[33] chronological-
ly the last of the English series, although it was written four years
before *Verre d'eau* and six years before *Fils de Cromwell*. It is a
close look at the question of power in itself; the moral values are
measured, but no real judgment is rendered in clearcut terms of
good and evil as in other works.

Set in the time of George II, the play centers on the remarkable
Robert Walpole, England's first Prime Minister and chief of the
Whig party for over twenty years. Walpole, who coined the phrase,
"Every man has his price," is a fiercely ambitious man who having
achieved the highest position, now feels his isolation from others.
His attempts to reach out on a human level lead him to renounce
his power, only to discover that he then cannot be content without
it. Scribe, amused at the dilemma, does not condemn Walpole;
rather, he seems to be saying that able men have an obligation to
use their talents, and that a denial of opportunity is tantamount to
death.

Unlike British historians, Scribe does not present Walpole as particularly corrupt, but rather as a skilled statesman who belongs at
the top. Corruption, for Scribe, apparently develops from the kind
of inherited power that is accountable to no one, here belonging to
the King and Lady Cecile, two completely self-centered characters
who place personal pleasure above the good of the country.
Walpole, on the other hand, is kept in control by his enemies and is
accountable to Parliament. He can be overthrown; indeed, is at one
point, when only the most strenuous exercise of his skill saves
him—and the country.

Scribe may not approve of royalty, but he is not unaware of its
effect on people. Walpole's friend, Neuboroug, is a fine doctor, living a perfectly contented life with his daughter until he is introduced to court life. In the first part, he appears to have a slight
but normal jealousy of his brilliantly successful friend whom he
charges with forgetting old ties. Once at court, however, he is
himself immediately infected with a lust for position that makes
Walpole's ambition seem almost innocent by contrast.

In fact, Walpole's desire for power is not unreasonable; he is
clearly the most capable person in the play. George II is weak and
self-indulgent, Walpole's nephew Eric is too naive and inexperi-

enced to deal with the complexities of state and court. Eric's love story forms the narrative line, and its happy conclusion is the comic resolution, but the central problem remains with Walpole and the realistic evaluation of the power structure.

XVII   *Metaphor for the Present*

It is obvious that, while Scribe uses historical backgrounds, his primary concerns are twofold: first, in the construction of a theatrically valid drama, second in the choice of subjects of value in his own time. The first consideration, unquestionably essential to the genre, often dictates the second. In the theater, a panoramic treatment of historical events usually means a disorganized, economically unfeasible pageant; a long view of a battle can be effective on film, but on the stage it is merely confusing, and, in a tightly constructed play, impossible. He therefore wisely chose the backstage approach consonant with his own interest in the individuals where a complex series of plot lines could be most fully exploited. To say the history of books is not involved here is not to say that this is without value. The very humanity of Scribe's characters overcomes the barriers of time and makes an Adrienne Lecouvreur, a Charles V or a Walpole as alive in the twentieth century as in an earlier time.

The approach obviates one outstanding disadvantage faced by every writer who attempts to fictionalize history: the lack of suspense. Most of the audience knows enough general facts to predict the outcome, and the normal avenues by which a writer keeps their attention are closed. Scribe does not rely on this kind of surprise, but develops suspense through intrigue and plot reversals that affect the fictitious characters, leaving history to follow its own inevitable path and himself free to produce surprises in the way events and characters sort themselves out.

To say he was uninterested in history is manifestly inexact. The plays themselves refute this, and a careful study reveals details that only an ardent student would be apt to know. These details are slipped casually into dialogue ostensibly concerned with other matters, but, although they may seem unimportant, they give depth and scope to the characters. As an added benefit, it might be mentioned that when the details are checked against biographies and standard histories, they almost always prove correct. Yet he adds another dimension of immense importance to the artist—and here he is at one with Shelley, who pointed to the inevitable weakness of the historian as compared to the poet:

The one is partial, and applies only to a definite period of time, and a certain combination of events which can never again recur; the other is universal, and contains within itself the germ of a relation to whatever motives or actions have place in the possible varieties of human nature.[34]

Such universality which gives the past an immediacy not found in dusty archives focuses the attention on those questions still being asked today. For Scribe, history is not a book of lessons, but a metaphor for the present.

CHAPTER 5

Scribe's Influence

I Scribe in France

SOME plays transfer most effectively from one country's stage to another. It is frequently the case, however, that a dramatist is so tied to his own culture, to his own particular audience, that such a transfer becomes difficult if not impossible. A playwright's success in his native land is not necessarily a guarantee of success on foreign soil.

Scribe, however, was able to transcend all national barriers, and his plays were to enjoy a success that embraced all of Europe. The result of this success was a significant influence on the developing theater not only of France but of the entire continent. Even those authors who, like Bernard Shaw, affected a certain scorn for Scribe, underwent a significant influence on the part of the French dramatist.

In France in the early nineteenth century, there were many authors writing plays, authors who have had their works much more readily classified as "literature." Alfred de Vigny, Victor Hugo, Alfred de Musset, Gerard de Nerval, Balzac all wrote plays. Many of these works which had a great temporary success, are in many cases reduced to the status of museum pieces today. Vigny's Shakespearean adaptations have now been superseded by more authentic approximations of the English originals, while his *Chatterton* is seen by today's reader as excessively Romantic and sentimental. The effect on modern theater audiences can only be conjectural: presentday revivals of the play are all but unknown.

Victor Hugo's plays such as *Ruy Blas* and *Hernani* enjoy occasional revivals today, but are acceptable only to the extent that the spectator is willing project himself back into the heroic and Romantic excesses of the 1830s. The plays are likewise handsome vehicles for stellar artists; but in such cases, it is the power of the

111

artist rather than the interest of the play itself which carries the work along. Hugo's *théâtre en liberté* offers at least as much contrast with his earlier plays as is to be found between *The Hunchback of Notre Dame* and *Les Misérables* in his novelistic work. The late plays, however, are more the subject of theoretical and literary investigations than living works of the theater.

Musset's dramas, perhaps the best plays of the first half of the nineteenth century, are dramatic books rather than plays: they were written to be read, for the most part, and can only be presented onstage in adaptations. Sarah Bernhardt scored impressive success in Musset, and in more recent times Gerard Philippe enjoyed enormous popularity in his work, but in both cases, the play as a virtuoso vehicle is the prime consideration. Certainly outside of France, Musset's plays are infrequently performed, although volumes of translations have had some success with the reading public.

Gerard de Nerval, in spite of his genius as a poet and prose writer, never seemed to achieve stature in the theater. (We must remember that some critics claimed Scribe was in part responsible for Nerval's suicide: by selfishly monopolizing the stage and not allowing younger authors [that is, Nerval] to achieve fame, he created the suicidal attitude, as was earlier discussed.) Nerval's closest approach to popular success was reached in a collaborative effort with Dumas.

Balzac's plays were likewise minor works compared to the great *Comédie humaine*. As in the case of Zola's plays at the end of the century, the works were a pale shadow of the novelistic achievements, and for the same reason: in both cases, the genius of the author is the descriptive genius, not the dramatic. The descriptive element has little place in a modern play.

Alexandre Dumas was a playwright as well as being a novelist. He was certainly more successful as a dramatic creator if we judge by the number of plays (which fill twenty-five volumes) and the number of performances throughout the years. Here again, though, if we compare the author's plays to his novels we find the novels infinitely superior.

Unlike these other authors, who seemed caught in the backwater eddy of exaggerated Romanticism for the most part, Scribe was in the main line of theatrical development. He is much more a descendent of Diderot and the new dramatic theories of the eighteenth century in France than were the others. But Scribe was not hampered as Diderot was by a lack of dramatic ability. Diderot's theories are admirable, but he was unable to put them into practice in a successful play. Scribe, building on many of these principles, was able to produce success after success.

Given this success, it is no wonder that future dramatic development stemmed mainly from Scribe. Sardou, continuing the tradition of the *pièce bien faite*, produced numerous successes, and the ultimate development of the techniques came with the farces of Feydeau, which, since 1950, have experienced a phenomenal popularity in his numerous revivals in France and the Anglo-Saxon world. Even the main exponent of the Naturalist school in drama, Becque, can be seen as a development of forces set in motion by Scribe, both in his serious plays *(Les Corbeaux)* and the lighter fare *(La Parisienne)*.

The situation outside of France is equally impressive. England, Spain, Germany, Russia, all fell under the spell of Scribe. A few important names can be cited: the influence of Scribe on Ibsen and Bernard Shaw is undeniable, although neither was particularly anxious to avow his debt, and Shaw in particular attempted to be harsh toward Scribe, perhaps further to obfuscate his debt.

It would be an endless task to try to delineate the full influence of Scribe on individual authors and his success in all of the Western European countries. The subjects have been dealt with, however, in varying degrees of detail in several works which have attempted to demonstrate either the popularity of Scribe's works in foreign lands or the influence he had on foreign authors.

II   *Spain*

The fate of Scribe in Spain, however, is the area which has been the least studied.[1] But this is not for lack of material. More than thirty plays were translated and presented. Madrid in particular seemed to be a center of activity for Scribe's plays. More than fifteen translators were involved in these adaptations, which consisted of both plays and *opéras-comiques*. The traditional Spanish *zarzuela*, of course is very close to the French *opéra-comique*, which fact may account for a great deal of the popularity enjoyed by the musical works—but the straight dramatic offerings had equal success.

The Spanish eighteenth century was not fertile with great dramatists. One can cite Moratín, but then the list is all but closed. The Spanish stage was therefore open to outside influences, and Scribe was the obvious figure to supply those influences.

Many of Scribe's Spanish translators are today relatively obscure or entirely unknown to anyone but the literary historian. Ramón de Arriola, Nicolas Lombra, Ramón de Navarrete, Juan del Peral, Isidoro Gil, Francesco Cologno, Gil de Zarate, D.G.F. Coll, Genaro Lino Zayati and Julián Romea are typical. The most prolific of the translators was Ventura de la Vega. He adapted at least thirteen plays for the Spanish stage. The public was thus exposed to a variety of Scribe plays presented by these translators. But there were also other translators who were themselves among the best known writers and dramatists of their day.

Mariano José de Larra translated *La Famille Riquebourg* (as *Partir a tiempo*). Larra (1809-1842) was the intellectual heir of Cadalso, the eighteenth-century author whose *Cartas marruecas* were at the fountainhead of the *costumbrista* movement in Spanish literature. Larra is best known today as one of the important writers in this genre who chose the essay as the vehicle for the study of manners. There are, of course, comparisons to be made with some of the earlier authors in the English tradition such as Addison and Steele in the *Spectator*, but this type of literature seems to have taken hold more firmly in Spain than elsewhere; and for some reason, the study of manners which in France and England came to be achieved mainly through the novel of manners, was in Spain kept in a purer essay form.

Given Larra's predilection for the study of manners, there is no surprise in his appreciation of Scribe's studies of manners in bourgeois France, as depicted in so many of his plays.

Another author, a dramatist, was the translator of *Batilde, o la America del Norte en 1775*. García Gutiérrez was popular in his time, but his Romantic tendencies, which somehow did not seem to take root in Spain, have relegated him to the second shelf. He is perhaps best remembered for his historical play, *La conjuración de Venecia* of 1834.

Probably the two greatest dramatic authors of the period in Spain were Juan Eugenio Hartzenbusch and Bretón de los Herreros. Both were involved in Scribe translations. Hertzenbusch appears to have translated only one play, curiously, *El abuelito* (*Le Bon Papa*). Bretón de los Herreros, on the other hand, did at least five plays, all for the Teatro del Príncipe in Madrid. He began in 1828 with *Un paseo a Bedlam* (*Une visite à Bedlam*), followed in 1831 by *Los primeros amores* (*Les Premières Amours*), *El segundo año* (*La Seconde Année*) in 1832, and *No más muchachas, o el solterón y la niña (Le Vieux Garçon et la petite fille). El amante prestado (Zoé, ou l'Amant prêté)* was also translated by Breton. It is of course difficult to say to what extent Scribe influenced Bretón and the others directly, and to what extent they merely found in him a kindred spirit who wrote plays which appealed to them, but with such an extended airing of his works, it seems inevitable that Scribe was to leave an enduring mark on the Spanish dramatists and public of the first half of the nineteenth century.

III England

In the English-speaking world, the influence of Scribe has been perpetuated through a long line of British dramatists whose writings indicate clear traces of the well-made play.[2] This does not mean these authors worshipped Scribe, or even particularly liked him, but that they recognized him, consciously or unconsciously, for the master craftsman of the theater he was.

Tom Robertson (1829 - 1871) wrote plays dealing with the Victorian middle class, painted in a very realistic manner. He had a thorough grounding in Scribe, and, in fact, he had adapted two of the latter's plays, *Ladies' Battle* and *The Glass of Water*, in the course of the 1850s—before achieving success later with his own plays. From Scribe, Robertson learned not only the mechanics of the well-made play, but also the realistic, nonrhetorical dialogue that so contrasted with classic theater. In another way, Robertson has a great deal of affinity with Scribe. Although Scribe was a writer and not a director, he was still very much involved in the practical side of theatrical presentation. Robertson was in fact a director and often had the opportunity of directing his own plays, much as Molière had done, so that the important details of transforming the play from the printed page to an actual production could be supervised with care. Scribe was always conscious of the desired visual effect, to the extent that he regularly indicated the relative position of each actor on the stage in the course of each scene's development. One of Robertson's scenes, the famed "snow scene" in *Ours*, recalls Scribe's ice-skating scene in *Le Prophète*. In Robertson, each time the door opened, a blast of snow would enter the stage. No doubt an effective scene at the time, as indicated by its constant repetition to the point of parody finally in one of the earlier W. C. Fields films (" 'Taint a fit night out for man nor beast!' ")

Sydney Grundy (1848 - 1914) was another author well trained in the Scribe tradition. He translated and adapted many plays by Scribe and later French dramatists, achieving notable success.

Henry Arthur Jones (1851 - 1929) did much to acclimate the *pièce bien faite* to the English stage. In the early years of the nineteenth century, there had been an enormous vogue for the Gothic melodramas such as *The Castle Spectre, The Vampire*, dramatizations of *Frankenstein* and the like.[3] This current had left a taste for the fantastic, the exaggerated, the extraordinary. Jones was prepared to offer the public something simpler. The contrast of Jones's plays with much of the prevailing taste prompted a critic to write:

The public are pining for a pure English comedy, with a pure story, in which the characters shall be English, with English ideas, and English feelings, honest, true men, and tender, loving women, and from which plague, pestilence, adultery, fornication, battle, murder, and sudden death may be banished.[4]

This list of forbidden topics would rule out some of the Scribe plays, such as *Adrienne Lecouvreur* with the murder of the actress, and many of the operas, *opéras-comiques* and vaudevilles, but certainly the main thrust of Scribe is toward a straightforward contemporary social study. Even in the historical plays, such as *The Glass of Water*, the historical element plays practically no part (indeed, Scribe feels free to invent his history where necessary), so that the work becomes a character study.

Jones, in adopting the careful dramatic technique of Scribe and his subject matter, had only to adapt the material to the English scene in order to produce a highly acceptable home-grown product.

Arthur Wing Pinero (1855 - 1934) must certainly be classed among the most important followers in the wake of Scribe, if we judge by the continued success in modern times of plays such as his *Trelawney of the Wells*, which has never failed to attract the public in a number of revivals.

In his *The Second Mrs. Tanqueray* (1893), we have a serious play (ending in the self-poisoning of the main character) in which the precepts of the well-made play are observed scrupulously, at least up to a point. Everything that happens, occurs naturally and necessarily:

The dramatist's job is to arrange things in such a way that his characters seem likely to do what he wants them to do, and preferably more likely to do than anything else.[5]

This technique is precisely what the *pièce bien faite* is all about, and to the extent that the precepts are followed by Pinero and others, the influence of Scribe can be said to continue.

Of course, the technique can appear to be too obvious, and for some, this renders the play detestable. Shaw, in particular, inveighed against *The Second Mrs. Tanqueray* for these reasons, and *a fortiori* against the plays of Scribe as well.

Others of Pinero's plays continued, to one extent or another, this adherence to the structure of the well-made play, with the frequent exception of the ending, which often departs from the logic and necessity characterized by Scribe, at least in the estimation of his critics.

Trelawney of the Wells (1898) is not particularly close to Scribe in style or technique, but it does recall *Adrienne Lecouvreur* by the realistic and highly sympathetic view of backstage life in the theater. *Trelawney*, however, as a comedy, both in form and plot is far different from Scribe.

The history of the well-made play can be traced further, through Bernard Shaw, Oscar Wilde, and on into the contemporary period. The influence is there, certainly, but diluted, and sometimes negative in nature: namely the playwrights' continuing revolt against the *pièce bien faite*. Finally all this is mixed with the many other influences current in the theater, with Ibsen of course in the forefront.

Since the seventeenth century at least, there has always been a close association between the British theater and the French. The mutual exchange of ideas, plots and techniques, has served to enrich both.

In turn, the British theater had its effect on the American scene, so that Scribe's influences were doubly felt—directly from Scribe adaptations—and indirectly from the English authors.

A good example of the American exponent of the *pièce bien faite* is Clyde Fitch (1865 - 1909), whose melodramas, *The Girl with Green Eyes* (1903) and *The Truth* (1907) bear the stamp of Scribe.

Shaw, although he was loath to admit it, was, as we have said, much under the influence of Scribe. Indeed, much of the influence may have been negative, but a great deal of it was also positive.

Moreover, not only did Shaw undergo the influence directly, but also much (although by no means most) of the innovation brought to the stage by Ibsen can be traced back to Scribe as well. Ibsen himself had been closely associated with Scribe's plays in the years between 1851 and 1856, when he directed no fewer than twenty-one Scribe plays at Bergen.

To a certain extent in subject matter, but particularly in the area of technique, Shaw exhibited the stamp of Scribe. A detailed analysis of such influences in plays such as *Candida, The Devil's Disciple, Captain Brassbound's Conversion* and *Man and Superman* has already been made and is quite convincing.[6]

IV   Scandinavia

Scandinavia was no stranger to Scribe's plays. Ibsen, in his Bergen period was merely reflecting the popular taste: Scandinavia shared with the other countries of Europe the adulation for the French author. The Scandinavian influence, however, was particularly important in view of two of the towering figures who were touched by it: Ibsen and Kierkegaard. As they were influenced themselves, so did they pass on the same influence—greatly modified, of course, by their own particular perceptions—but passed on nonetheless.

Certainly Ibsen is one of the major figures in drama. As already mentioned in connection with Shaw, Ibsen spent the years between 1851 and 1856 in Bergen directing plays. Of the seventy or so he directed, twenty-one of them were Scribe plays. This gives an excellent picture of the relative importance of Scribe in the international repertory. One can only envy the citizenss of Bergen, for their opportunity of seeing more than seventy plays in the space of five years, all directed by Ibsen.

A director can be, and often is, dissatisfied with the plays he directs. He may even be driven to rewrite the play, make additions, add or delete characters as suits his fancy, but the fact remains that the director usually is conscious of some kind of value in the play he is directing, otherwise he would have chosen another play. It is true that a director may have to consider popular taste if he is to draw audiences to see his work, but within this restriction he normally has a free hand.

Ibsen, then, must have seen some merit in the Scribe plays. The fabled Scribe technique certainly was an important factor in Ibsen's dramatic development. Scribe's subject matter, likewise, the study of ordinary people in difficult situations, was certainly congenial to Ibsen's own turn of mind. He did not end up as an imitation Scribe; his development of the idea play goes far beyond Scribe. No one seems ever to have been scandalized by a Scribe play—he was confined too closley within the bourgeois morality for that. Ibsen, on the other hand, was a constant source of concern in "well-thinking" circles.

But for all his innovation, Ibsen still bore the mark of Scribe, and without the well-made play as a background, Ibsen might well have written in a rather different manner.

Ibsen had to overcome the initial scandal element, but once that was accomplished, or indeed partly because of it, his audience became as universal as Scribe's had ever been. As Shaw put it, after Ibsen, whether one liked him or not, one could never again see an oldfashioned play. We must not assume from this that Shaw was casting out Shakespeare and Molière, or even necessarily all of Scribe, but the theater had certainly turned a corner and entered upon a new era. This is not exclusively due to Ibsen, of course. The attitude was clear in Pinero's *Trelawney of the Wells*, which was not written under the influence of Ibsen; but it is still clear that, as seen from the inside, the theater was undergoing a change, becoming more serious, abandoning the old ways. The young actors were eager to accept the new aesthetic; the older ones could not change and dropped by the wayside. The same phenomenon occurred with the playwrights.

However, the influence of Scribe was passed on not only by the universal reputation of Ibsen's plays. In a more generalized way, the philosopher Kierkegaard was also a force in the spreading of Scribe.[7]

Some surprising statistics are quoted by the chroniclers of the Danish theater,[8] concerning Scribe performances in Copenhagen. Between 1825 and 1889, seventy-two of Scribe's plays were presented, for a total of 1500 performances. To give some perspective, during the adult lifetime of Kierkegaard (1829 - 1855), there were produced in Copenhagen more than one hundred performances of Scribe, compared to one hundred twenty-three for Molière. In addition, there were frequent performances of the Scribe operas, six hundred forty-one performances were given of the six most popular of the operas and *opéras-comiques;* in all, twenty-eight different operas were presented.

Scribe thus continues the phenomenon of transferability which so often limits the playwright to his native shores. But the importance of Scribe in the work of Kierkegaard is far more than a mere litany of performances and productions. The critics often maintain that all is form in Scribe, and that there is no substance. On the contrary, Kierkegaard mentions Scribe frequently in his works, sometimes to mention attending a performance (perhaps initially even in the original French: there were visiting French companies), but more frequently to illustrate a philosophical or psychological point. Kierkegaard was convinced that there was a very great authenticity in Scribe's character portrayals. He felt he could see in the theatrical characters the illustration of the same points he wished to make in his own writings on the subject of human nature.

V   Eastern Europe

Other foreign penetrations of Scribe have not been so carefully studied as those in England and Scandinavia, but there are some beginnings of such a study for Eastern Europe.[9] This study reveals an astonishing popularity of Scribe, even under the Soviet regime, which might well have been expected to despise the bourgeois attitudes of such a society as Scribe portrays.

VI   Germany

Scribe attained similar popularity in Germany. Parodies of some of his works were presented, and since a parody is understandable only in the context of a well-known model, Scribe was obviously well known to the public at large. One of the parodies of *The Glass of Water*, produced in Berlin, was entitled *A Glass of White Beer*.

The reception of Scribe by the German public has been the subject of a lengthy study.[10] Throughout the German-speaking area, Berlin, Leipzig, Vienna, performances abounded. More than one hundred twenty-five plays were produced in German. In addition, there appeared not only numerous publications of single plays by Scribe in German translation but also Scribe plays in several anthologies and a multivolume edition of Scribe's best-known plays in their German versions.

Scribe was not just a French author, but a world-wide phenomenon. His plays and operas held the stage throughout the world, seeming to respond to the tastes of every culture. It is little wonder that such unparalleled success excited the envy of his fellow authors. There are certainly many other examples of playwrights whose efforts have been successful throughout Europe and America, but seldom if ever did anyone by sheer quantity—and by quality too—reach such a vast audience.

It is easy to say that with the coming of Ibsen, the theater could never again return to the simple *pièce bien faite* of Scribe, but it is equally true that when Scribe came on the scene, he just as effectively transformed the theater of his predecessors.

CHAPTER 6

Scribe and Music

I The Musical Genres

S CRIBE'S involvement with music is in three areas: the ballet, *opéra-comique* and the opera. Centering his activities on the Paris Opera, Scribe nevertheless ventured farther afield at times and worked for Brussels and even London. All the famous composers, as can be seen in the huge collection of letters directed to Scribe which is housed in the Bibliothèque Nationale in Paris, were clamoring for his libretti and scenarios.

The most important of the musical works are the operas; some of the most significant operas of the time were written to Scribe libretti.

As for the *opéras-comiques,* at least one of them, *La Dame Blanche,* will be dealt with along with the operas. The more serious of them differ from the operas only in the inclusion of some spoken dialogue between the musical numbers. Other facets of the *opéras-comiques* have been treated with the plays, since the considerations are much the same in either case.

The ballets, however, call for some commentary. The nineteenth century was a time when many serious literary figures wrote the scenarios for ballets. The most famous of these was Théophile Gautier, the young Turk of the French Romantic movement.

At first glance, it might be considered that the scenario for a ballet is not a serious literary undertaking. Today's ballet goer is accustomed to ballets which have only the vaguest kind of story line. This might be the conclusion drawn also from an examination of Scribe's sketchy instructions for the opera ballets which occur in his operas; usually these are merely fragmentary suggestions to the choreographer.

However, a glance at any of the scenarios for the independent ballets will show quite the contrary. A good example is *Marco Spada*, with music composed by Auber. *Marco Spada* is noteworthy in that it is the only independent ballet to a scenario by Scribe which has been recorded (London CS6923, London Symphony, Bonynge). The only other ballet by Scribe with any currency is *The Skaters (Les Patineurs)* part of the American Ballet Theatre repertory, a frequently recorded item (music by Meyerbeer); but this is one of the opera ballets from *Le Prophète* and does not fit into our category of ballets with a significant story line.

II   *The Ballet of* Marco Spada

Marco Spada (1852) is the tale of a bandit. The governor of Rome and his daughter are sheltered by the bandit, who conceals his identity. The governor's daughter, the Marchesa, is betrothed to Frederici, but she loves another. In the course of the stay in the bandit's lair, Angela, Spada's daughter, falls in love with Frederici, and her love is returned. Spada and his daughter are invited to the governor's ball. It is there that Angela realizes that as a bandit's daughter she cannot marry Frederici. In the course of the ball, Spada's men abduct the Marchesa. Spada orders her to marry her lover Pepinelli, leaving the way free for Angela and Frederici. The governor's men have pursued the bandits and a battle ensues in which Spada is given a death blow. He then clears the last obstacle from Angela's marriage by declaring that in reality she is not his daughter.

This outline does not do justice to the considerable complications of the plot. Suffice it to say that Scribe here, as in his other scenarios, is extremely specific in his indications of actions—to the point of including dialogue for the dancers—which had, of course, to be conveyed by pantomime.

The ballet scenario then in fact, becomes, a literary subgenre with a plot indistinguishable from that of many contemporary plays.

An anecdote illustrates the attention which the nineteenth-century balletgoer paid to the subtleties of plot. According to Scribe's friend and colleague, Legouvé, one day the director of the Opera appeared at Scribe's door, distraught. It seems that a new ballet which had been in rehearsal for some time was about to be presented. But only at the last minute had the director become aware of an impossible contradiction in the plot. It seems that in the first act the prima ballerina is given a magic talisman which is all-powerful. But in the second act she is called on to organize the members of the harem to revolt against their slavery. The inconsistency, as seen by the director, was that if she had a magic talisman, there was no need to organize the others for an attack. Could Scribe find a way out of this dilemma? After a few moments of thought, Scribe suggested that at the end of the first act the ballerina should fall asleep on the grass. A young shepherd, in love with the ballerina, could steal up and take the talisman (a rose) from her; thus the need for organizing the revolt was justified.

Although one wonders how many of the members of the audience would actually bother to worry about such inconsistencies, the anecdote nevertheless illustrates the dramatic consistency and precision which Scribe and his audience demanded of the contemporary ballet.

The ballet scenarios which tend to be somewhat more likely to deal in fantasy than the straight dramatic plays, frequently involve the typical Romantic themes of the times. On the whole, however, they betray the same dramatic considerations and techniques that Scribe used in the rest of his work.

III   The Operas

One of Scribe's major claims to fame stems, or should stem, from his activity as an author of opera libretti. His role here, however, has never, for a number of reasons, been properly assessed. On the one hand, although many music scholars recognize the importance of the libretto, many others tend to discount the importance of the text in their evaluation of the work as a whole. Literary scholars are even more guilty, tending to disregard opera libretti as entirely unworthy of consideration. This is unfortunate in a genre which the French eighteenth century saw as the ideal combination of all the arts—literature, dance, music, painting.

When literary scholars do give attention to opera libretti, it is perhaps even more unfortunate, because they judge a libretto as if it were a play. Using these standards, few libretti are of a nature appropriate to stand up to such comparison. A good opera may well come from an adaptation of a good play, but a good play does not by any means guarantee a good opera will come from it. The nature of opera is such that it requires a different kind of literary piece from the straight dramatic play or simple comedy. In short, the text must always be interpreted in conjunction with the music, and the final test of a libretto has to be how well it serves the composer both in inspiring and in giving him the opportunity to develop his musical potential.

Thus, as with the other genres in which Scribe dealt, in the opera it has also become traditional for critics to sneer and declare Scribe worthless and incompetent. This, however, ignores facts. Scribe was involved with practically every composer of any importance in his day: Auber, Boieldieu, Cherubini, Clapisson, Donizetti, Gounod, Halévy, Meyerbeer, Offenbach, Rossini, Thomas, Verdi and Weber.

The extent of his collaboration varied from work to work. In some cases, he was the sole author of the libretto to which the opera was composed. Sometimes the subjects were original, sometimes they were adaptations of works of literature. At times Scribe worked in collaboration with one or more other librettists. At times, Scribe's intervention came only later, such as in the adaptation of foreign works for the French Opera. But even in these last cases, the role of Scribe was significant. One of the best documented examples is to be found in the collaboration on Donizetti's *Poliuto*, based on Corneille's seventeenth-century tragedy, *Polyeucte*.

The Italian opera was composed for the Teatro San Carlo in Naples, although the severe censorship then reigning in the Italian states prevented its presentation. The censor decreed that the subject was too sacred (it concerned the death of the early Christian martyr) to be displayed on an opera stage. Donizetti, under contract to present an opera in Paris, decided to adapt *Poliuto* for that purpose. For the adaptor he chose Scribe, and, although it was merely a new version of an already existing work, Donizetti tells us how important he considered this reworking to be:

At the French Grand Opera I'll give my *Poliuto*, banned in Naples because of being too sacred, lengthened to four acts instead of three as it was, and translated and adjusted for the French theatre by Scribe. For that reason, it comes to pass that I have had to make all the recitatives, write a new finale for Act I, add arias, trios, and such related ballets as they use here, so that the public may not complain that the "tessitura" is Italian, in which they make no mistake. French music and theatrical poetry have a cachet all their own, to which every composer must conform, whether in the recitatives or in the sung numbers . . . between one *cabaletta* and another they always have poetry that intensifies the action without the repetition of lines which our poets are accustomed to use.[1]

It is clear that Scribe, even entering the project at the eleventh hour, had a profound effect on the final form the opera was to take. It is significant that Donizetti is apparently content to accept Scribe as the arbiter of what is acceptable to the French audience.

Another fact that is often disregarded: not only did Scribe's operatic activity extend to all of the important composers, but it covered an extensive period as well. Scribe's operas were written over a period of more than thirty years. Logic compels us to believe that the composers were getting what they wanted from him. How else can we explain their constant return to him for new libretti? Auber composed a dozen operas to Scribe scores. Halévy did a half-dozen Scribe operas. Meyerbeer did four.

The importance of Scribe's role is all the greater since several of the particular works involved are among the monuments of operatic history. Even a cursory glance at music criticism of this period reveals that everything is judged in terms of Auber's *La Muette de Portici*, Boieldieu's *La Dame blanche*, Meyerbeer's *Les Huguenots*, *Le Prophète* and *Robert le diable*, and Halévy's *La Juive*. The role of Meyerbeer in revolutionizing the opera of his time is well known. Some may maintain that all this was the result exclusively of Meyerbeer's talents, but a more reasoned interpretation suggests that the texts to which he composed his operas played a significant part in that revolution.

Many of these operas, having passed from style, as a result are not currently presented. Styles in music, however, have a tendency to return, and this is certainly the case with many of the Scribe operas. Successful revivals of Meyerbeer's operas, Weber's *Freischuetz*, Rossini's *Comte Ory*, Donizetti's *Favorita*, are only a few of those that have found renewed favor recently.

IV   *The Nature of the Libretti*

In speaking of opera, it is perhaps necessary to confront the distinction between opera and *opéra-comique*. For our purposes here, we are considering for the most part only the operas. The *opéras-comiques* tend to be of less value and interest. However, the distinction is rather artibrary: the opera contains no spoken dialogue, while the *opéra-comique* contains spoken dialogue of greater or lesser importance according to the individual case. Bizet's *Carmen*, for example, is technically an *opéra-comique* (to which sung recitative was composed at a later date to allow it to become an "opera"). In the same way, some of the more serious of Scribe's *opéras-comiques* can be considered along with the true operas without fear of distortion.

What is the distinction that needs to be made between a play and an opera libretto? The difference is at least as great as that between a novel and a play. In a novel, there is contact between the author and the reader without any intermediary. With a play, there is a group of interpreters placed between the author and the public: actors, directors, designers, lighting technicians. All must work well and in harmony to create a success.

In an opera, to a far greater extent than in a play or novel, there is an immediate and direct transferral of emotion. The main vehicle for this emotion is the music. An opera libretto must therefore be painted in much broader strokes, along much simpler lines in order to serve the music best. The nuances are the role of the music, not the text. A text filled with philosophical and psychological fine points will hinder rather than help the musician. The text must serve not only as a framework but as an inspiration. It must be reducible to the broad lines of a synopsis, since even if the opera is given in the language of the spectators, the words are largely unintelligible. We must remember that in the Gilbert and Sullivan operas, where the words were of paramount importance, printed libretti were always made available to the audience. Puns and satire often do not come across well with a musical presentation.

Another requisite of the opera libretto is to allow the kind of development expected by the eighteenth-century theorists: the opera must be a combination of all the arts. Thus, if there are no grand scenes (such as the coronation scene from *Le Prophète)* to feast the eyes, if there is no occasion for a ballet, the spectacle is necessarily incomplete.

It is in this area of supplying the composer with a framework, and giving him the potential for the grand visual evocations, that Scribe excels.

V   La Dame Blanche

La Dame blanche [The Lady in White] is the first of Scribe's great musical successes. It was first performed in 1825 at the theatre of the Opéra-Comique in Paris. The music was by Boieldieu. It became an immediate success, a part of everyone's musical heritage. Allusions to the work abound not only in musical criticism, but even in literature: in Henri Becque's play, *Les Corbeaux*, [The Ravens,] the monument of Naturalist theater in France, M. Vanderk invites his daughter to sing an air from *La Dame blanche*. The music has now passed from fashion, and revivals of the work are rare, but some numbers survive as concert pieces and on records.

The work is an *opéra-comique* with substantial dialogue. The scene is set in Scotland. At the time of the composition, Scotland had a firmly founded reputation as a home for elves and spirits. Along with the literary hoax of the poems of Ossian, which popularized the Celtic legends and locales, a more recent work, *Trilby, or the Elf of Argyll*, had been published[2] only three years before the premiere of *La Dame blanche*. Although the works have nothing in common but the locale and the suggestion of the supernatural, Scribe no doubt had *Trilby* in mind as he was writing—a fact made obvious by the use of Trilby for the subject of one of his plays.

This, then, was the background Scribe was to exploit for the opera libretto. George, a young lieutenant, arrives in a village where he is greeted by the tenants of the lord of Avenel, who for his having supported the Stuarts was exiled from Scotland. George is an orphan with unknown background. The estate manager for Avenel, Gaveston, has returned to the castle to preside over its sale, to pay off the Avenel debts. He intends to purchase the castle himself, thus taking over both the property and the title of his former master. Gaveston, who expects no competitors at the auction, is certain of getting a bargain. But one of the farmers, who when once at the point of ruin is supposed to have been saved by the Lady in White, receives a note from the spectre demanding his presence. He is afraid, so George offers to replace him at the rendezvous. The Lady in White is actually Anna, in disguise. Anna, an orphan raised by the Avenel family, is now the ward of Gaveston. She wishes to foil his plans and so asks obedience from George. This obedience is assured because Anna holds a secret power over him: she was the mysterious young lady who nursed George back to health after he had been wounded on the battlefield. They had fallen in love, but she had been obliged to follow Gaveston and desert George.

The Justice of the Peace arrives for the sale. There is first a competition between a group of farmers and Gaveston, where Gaveston easily outbids them. Then Anna delivers to George the orders of the Lady in White. George, although without any resources, must outbid Gaveston. After he does, George is informed that he must pay the total sum before noon or risk prison. He has implicit faith that the Lady will provide; Anna had been informed by Lady d'Avenel before her death, that the family fortune was hidden in the statue of the White Lady. Anna enters with the chest holding the fortune (in banknotes, in order to occupy a minimum of space) and the day is saved. She now feels herself unworthy of marrying George, a great Lord, but he insists, and all ends happily.

The story is both complicated and simple. There is a great amount of detail, and yet at the same time the spectator is in good position to guess the true identity of George from almost the very beginning. The detail is useful in lending proper motivation and credibility. The transparent plot adds to the enjoyment of the spectator. There is no complicated plot whose solution is a mystery. On the contrary, we enjoy the intrigue all the more in that we know as spectators things the participants do not yet know. We are interested not in what the outcome will be, but rather in the way the outcome is achieved. It is precisely the details of the plot and action which make the story line convincing as it moves from step to step.

No true supernatural exists here. The influence of the Ann Radcliffe tradition of the Gothic novel is obvious (Mrs. Radcliffe's novel, *The Mysteries of Udolpho*, served as the subject for another of Scribe's plays.) Characteristically, in Mrs. Radcliffe's work, a seemingly supernatural series of events ultimately has its own logical explanation.

To give but one example of the use of detail to justify the action, we may examine the final scene. Anna has declared that she and old Margaret, the servant, will flee immediately after saving the castle from Gaveston, because as a poor orphan she can never become the Countess of Avenel. Her final appearance will be as the Lady. The dramatic problem to solve is how to let George know that the Lady is Anna and how to force Anna to accept George's proposal. Scribe achieves this in an admirable fashion: as the Lady is departing, everyone is awed by her presumably supernatural presence, and defers. All except Gaveston, who, furious at having been undone, attacks the "phantom." He tears away her veil, revealing her to be Anna. The way is clear then for George to protest his love and end the opera happily.

There are many other advantages which Scribe, as the librettist, brings to this opera. The settings, of great potential visual beauty, correspond to many of the current fashions. There are three settings: the first act is in the farmhouse, behind which can be seen the mountains of the highland countryside. Both the pastoral life and mountain scenery were of great sentimental attraction to audiences of this period. Act Two is a Gothic hall in the castle. The revival of interest in Gothic architecture was a phenomenon which had grown throughout the eighteenth century to become at the beginning of the nineteenth a veritable fascination. Not only do we see the Gothic hall, but frequent reference is made to the ruins of an even older castle which the Gothic one replaced. The poetry of ruins was another theme which had reached prominence by the end of the eighteenth century. The third act is another room in the castle, equally laden with Gothic overtones. Both rooms are replete with hidden passageways, another favorite element of Romantic popular literature.

Finally, the texts that Scribe composed for the musical numbers are ideal. French is notoriously difficult to set to music, because of the lack of a strong fixed accent in the language. Scribe, however, is extremely innovative in his use of language. The melodic element of his poetry is often so very pronounced that it cries out for a musical setting. Many of the techniques Scribe uses are the ones usually associated with Victor Hugo, who is generally looked upon as an innovator, in spite of the fact that his poetry was for the most part of a later date than the libretto for *La Dame blanche*. We may go even further. It was Verlaine in his *Art poétique* who recommended the use of poetic lines composed of an uneven number of syllables as being of greater musicality. Many years earlier, Scribe was doing this very thing: some of his verses are of the very unusual length of five syllables.

The dominant form of French poetry is the alexandrine verse, which is composed of twelve syllables with a caesura in the middle. Although in this type of poetry there is a secondary caesura which may vary in position inside each of the half-lines, this form can tend to be prosaic (hence the almost absolute necessity of rhyme in French poetry). The effect is intensified if the alexandrine is set to music. Scribe uses many alexandrine verses, to be sure, but the rhythm is varied by the use of many other forms, particularly the eight-syllable line, and on occasion, rareties such as the five-syllable line. The aria "Viens, gentille dame," for example, is written in couplets formed of five-syllable lines:

> Viens, gentille dame;
> Ici, je reclame

La foi des serments;
A tes lois fidèle,
Me voici, ma belle;
Paris, je t'attends![3]

Lest this unusual form become annoying, Scribe shifts to a six-syllable line for the verse:

Que ce lieu solitaire
Et que ce doux mystère
Ont des charmes pour moi!
Oui, je sens qu'à ta vue
L'âme doit être émue;
Mais ce n'est pas d'effroi.[4]

Then comes a return to the five-syllable refrain. In the verse, the rhyme scheme *aabccb* adds notably to the rhythmic effect, *a* and *c* being long, sustained vowels, and *b* short.

With such a text, we would expect the composer to be inspired. Indeed, this air, along with "Quel plaisir d'être soldat" from the first act, is one of the most famous pieces in the opera.

The Lady in White, then, in all ways illustrates admirably Scribe's talent for producing precisely what is needed to form a foundation for the music. At the same time, the language has precisely the tone required. It suggests a natural conversation, while keeping track of the need for a more elevated tone to go along with a musical setting. It is no wonder that after such a success with *La Dame blanche*, Scribe's services were so much in demand.

VI Le Comte Ory

It is difficult to know exactly what to say about *Le Comte Ory* which Scribe prepared for Rossini for a premiere in August of 1828. Certainly it is a far different work from the grand operas written for Halévy and Meyerbeer. Two things appear to determine the difference: first, the libretto grew out of a vaudeville which Scribe had written earlier. Second, although in his French period Rossini was for the most part writing serious operas such as *William Tell*, the comic genius of Rossini was eminently suitable for a light work of this sort.

Count Ory himself is an ambiguous character: in part he is the vile seducer, but as is so often the case with a Don Juan figure, he takes on a kind of bravura that makes him enviable. Here, of course, the figure is given a comic treatment, so that despite the black undertones, there is almost continual good humor.

Count Ory is the wastrel son of a nobleman who appears to spend his time seeking out the beautiful wenches of twelfth-century Touraine. For the moment, he is masquerading as a soothsayer in the village near the Countess' castle, dispensing advice to all who will listen. The Countess herself comes to seek this advice, which the Count willingly gives, attempting to further his own suit with the lady. As he is about to take her into the castle, however, his father's men arrive and unmask him, ending the first act. In the second, the Count and his men disguise themselves as pilgrim nuns and gain access to the castle, the Countess having taken pity on them, given the tempestuous weather outside. The Count uses his disguise to penetrate the Countess' chamber; but meanwhile, Isolier, the Count's page and a cousin of the Countess, has arrived to announce the imminent return of the men of the castle who have been away at the Crusades. Isolier, who realizes who the "nuns" are, disguises himself as the Countess, so that when the Count, disguised as "Sister Colette," attempts to make love to the "Countess," it is actually to Isolier.

When the men of the castle arrive, the Count and his men beat a hasty retreat after learning of Isolier's trick.

The plot is not particularly ingenious, and the ending has been criticized for its lack of imagination. It serves admirably for the opera, however. For that matter, many of the great French comedies (one thinks of *Tartuffe*) are resolved by *dénouements* which are no more satisfactory.

Several aspects are reminiscent of earlier works: certain parts of the story recall Rousseau's opera, *Le Devin du village* in which the village soothsayer gives advice on matters of love to Colin and Colette. (The scene reappears in Mozart's *Bastien und Bastienne* which was modeled on the Rousseau piece). There are also echoes of *Don Giovanni*, not only in the attitudes of the Count which resemble greatly those of the Don, but even to the similarities of the role of the Tutor of the Count who bemoans his lot much as does Don Giovanni's servant Leporello in the aria "Notte e giorno faticar . . ." Finally, the disguise of Isolier recalls *The Marriage of Figaro*.

Although most would not agree with the assessment, some critics have called *Count Ory* the masterpiece of Rossini. But it is certain that late in his career, when the opera was composed, he was at the summit of his powers. Verdi's *Aida* is perhaps much more popular than his *Falstaff,* although most would agree that the latter opera is greatly superior. Perhaps the same could be said of this and other Rossini operas. Certainly, Scribe supplied the composer with the material for a masterpiece.

In the first act there is an admirable patter song sung by various characters who tell the soothsayer what they want ("Moi je réclame / Pour que ma femme / Dans mon ménage / Soit toujours sage . . ."). A Gilbert and Sullivan patter song perhaps best describes the nature of such a piece:

This particularly rapid, unintelligible patter
Isn't generally heard, and if it is it doesn't matter[5]

And indeed, much of the singing is, as expected, unintelligible. Patter songs are frequent in the Italian opera *(Figaro, Dr. Bartolo, Dr. Dulcamara)* but much less so in French. With his gift for the manipulation of language, Scribe manages to write words which may rival in sound any of the complexities of the Italian arias.

As far as the action is concerned, there are the stock comic characters such as the (prefeminist) deceiver of women, and the trickster who is himself tricked. But it is the second act which offers the two scenes capable of the most complete comic development. The rough soldiers masquerading as nuns provide an immediate source of visual comedy. The scene is heightened by the situation in which Scribe places them: left alone with their bottles, they break into a riotous drinking song. A woman of the castle is heard approaching, and they immediately kneel, intoning a pious prayer. The lady is duly impressed and moves on, whereupon the "nuns" again break out with their ribald drinking song.

Finally, a delightful scene is procured by the disguise of Isolier as the Countess. (One thinks of Mozart's *Marriage of Figaro* with the disguises of Cherubino and the mutual exchange of costumes between Suzanna and the Countess Almaviva). The spectacle of the overamorous Count trying to make love to his own page is perfectly designed to keep the audience at a high level of amusement.

Scribe's success in this libretto is all the more impressive given the circumstances of composition: the second act comes from the earlier vaudeville play; but also, Rossini, making use of leftovers, wanted to incorporate into this opera long passages from his earlier unsuccessful opera *Viaggio a Reims*. The cohesion of the final libretto is a tribute to the ingenuity of Scribe.

VII   Robert le Diable

Written for Meyerbeer, the libretto for *Robert le diable* was based on the inspirations of the Gothic novel and theater whose influence had reigned in France from the late eighteenth century on. The opera was first produced in 1831 at the Paris Opera. Scribe was well-acquainted with the major English works of the genre. M.G. Lewis's novel, *The Monk*, was to serve as the basis for his libretto for *La Nonne sanglante* with music by Gounod; Ann Radcliffe's *Mysteries of Udolpho* was to form the subject of a play; and in the present opera, the character Bertram is obviously reminiscent of Maturin's tragedy of *Bartram*.

Scribe does not imitate the manner of Ann Radcliffe here. The English author always took care in her novels to explain away, in the end, what mysterious occurrences had taken place by assigning perfectly logical and comprehensible causes. Scribe rather participated in the school of the "fantastic taken seriously" a doctrine which Charles Nodier not only advocated but practiced in his own tales. This serious school of the fantastic took the supernatural at face value, presenting it as implicitly real with no attempt to explain away the mystery. From the very beginning, opera had frequently dealt with mythology and the supernatural, so this tendency in Scribe is scarcely surprising.

Although in modern times the supernatural has been long relegated to a minor place in literature, recent works have begun again to exploit this matter. Indeed, the portrayal of a character as a child of the devil seems to have taken on particular popularity.

In *Robert le diable*, then, we are quite literally dealing with the son of the Devil. Robert is the product of the seduction of a virtuous young woman by the Devil. As portrayed by Scribe, this son inherits the two "characters"—"virtue" from his mother and "evil" from his father. There is a constant struggle between these two natures. The evil nature is particularly dominant in the presence of Robert's companion, Bertram.

The action takes place in Palermo. As in Ann Radcliffe's *Udolpho* and *The Italian*, there seems in the public mind to be some association of this type of action and Italy. Robert has been driven from his native Normandy through the evil reputation the diabolical half of his character has created. When Raimbaut and Alice, Norman peasants, arrive, Robert, who first allows his evil nature to reign, threatens them. But upon recognizing Alice as his *soeur de lait*, that is, the daughter of his wet nurse, protects the couple from the assembled rakes and reprobates who sing the praises of pleasure and drink.

Robert loves the local princess, Isabelle, and the affection is returned; but the king has promised her hand to the winner of a tournament, who is expected to be the Prince of Granada. To be more certain, the Prince lures Robert into a kind of enchanted forest where he will wander until the tournament is over.

Bertram comes upon Robert in the forest. To assure his hold over the young man, he sets Robert a task: he must go to the convent and in the burial yard pluck a certain branch from a grave which will give him magical powers. Bertram reveals that Robert is indeed the son of the Devil, and that he, Bertram, is the Devil himself. He must assure himself of Robert's allegiance before midnight or lose him.

Bertram precedes Robert to the graveyard where he conjures up the souls of all the dead nuns, exhorting them to use their wiles to entrap Robert, in a kind of St. Anthony temptation. This they do when Robert appears, until on the point of submitting, he plucks the branch. But Alice appears with a letter from Robert's mother, written on her deathbed. She warns Robert against Bertram. This memory of his mother is sufficient to give ascendancy to the better part of his nature. He breaks the branch, denies Bertram, and is forgiven. The stage opens, revealing the interior of the Cathedral of Palermo where Isabelle and the entire court are assembled. Isabelle, Alice and the chorus intone:

> Glory, immortal glory
> To the God of the universe.
> He has remained faithful!
> The gates of heaven are open to him.[6]

This was one of the most successful of French operas in its time. The public was delighted with the supernatural subject matter, with the strong emotions, with the impressive scenery, not to mention the ballet of the enchanted nuns.

VIII   La Juive

La Juive, with music by Halévy, was first performed at the Paris Opera on February 28, 1835. While it was still in production, a critic wrote of the work:

A single fact, which is not common knowledge, and perhaps the one literary fact of the week, is a piquant and admirable meeting of artists, singers and men of letters, which took place this week with the Director of the Opera. They arrived early, and all the beautiful ladies were exact in their rendezvous with the arts. So they executed, *en famille* selections from the opera of the day, *La Juive*, of Mr. Halévy. The pieces sung by Nourrit, Levasseur and Miss Falcoz, are admirable. Meyerbeer, the great judge, who was there, couldn't sleep all night for having heard them . . .[7]

The opera did indeed go on to be the opera of the day, and long ruled as one of the masterpieces of nineteenth-century opera. Modern presentations, however, have been infrequent, in spite of great enthusiasm for the role of Eléazar by many famous tenors.

Once again Scribe shows his mastery of the medium. His libretto is admirably suited both to the musical and the visual needs of the work. The story is relatively simple, avoiding the pitfalls of many operas whose stories are excessively complicated to the point of making it impossible for the audience to follow what is occurring on the stage.

Eléazar is a rich Jewish goldsmith, living with his daughter, Rachel, in Constance in 1414 at the time of the Council of Constance. The followers of Huss have just been defeated by Prince Leopold. The conquering hero, however, has fallen in love with Rachel; he has been calling himself Samuel and pretending to be Jewish. As the Jewish community is celebrating Passover, Samuel/Leopold is unable to bring himself to eat the unleavened bread. Later, when the decisive moment comes, Leopold cannot abjure his Christian faith to marry Rachel. Rachel, furious, denounces him to the authorities. Both he and Rachel are then destined for the boiling cauldron. Rachel, however, prevailed upon to repent her denunciation of Leopold, says that her accusations were untrue; she loved Leopold, but he did not love her. He is therefore banished, while Rachel and her father Eléazar are to be sent to the cauldron. Rachel goes first, and as she dies, Eléazar, for revenge, informs Cardinal Brogni that Rachel was in fact born a Christian and was the Cardinal's daughter, who presumably had been massacred in Rome long ago before Brogni had taken holy orders.

All the requirements for a grandiose spectacle are present. The famous event, the Council of Constance, offers an impressive historical background and motivates a triumphant procession of the notables as the Council opens. Scribe gives special attention to this procession, noting in the stage directions the precise order and composition of the cortege.

The proposed settings, too, are admirably suited for the composition of a great spectacle. One can imagine the enthusiasm the set designer would feel in reading Scribe's directions for Act I:

An intersection in the city of Constance in 1414. On the right is the portal of a church. On the left, a street corner, with the shop of a goldsmith. Several fountains.

At the rise of the curtain, the portals of the church are open. The people who have not been able to enter the church are kneeling on the steps. In the middle of the square, men and women walk about; on the left, in front of the shop, Eléazar stands with his daughter Rachel. In the church the great choir is singing: *Te Deum Laudamus.*[8]

The detail of the fountains is important. They will serve in another scene especially successful from the visual point of view. In celebration of the victory over the Hussites, the Emperor has ordered that the fountains flow with wine. When this is accomplished, the people rush up in a wild scene of enjoyment and eventually drunkenness, which serves as a kind of comic relief from the serious considerations of the main plot. Drinking scenes are always a great success in opera: *Faust, Traviata, Cavalleria Rusticana* are only a few of the obvious examples.

Settings for the other acts are equally promising: Act II takes place in Eléazar's dwelling, where Passover is being celebrated. This too lends itself to a fascinating depiction of ethnic ceremony which no doubt captivated its audience, just as many of Delacroix's paintings had fascinated viewers with their portrayal of Jewish and Moslem ceremonies.

Act III is a splendid banquet scene. Act IV is a Gothic apartment in the castle. Act V is a vast tent (supported by Gothic columns), with the center of attention the boiling cauldron of bronze, into which the two victims are to be thrown.

As always, Scribe's ear is most sensitive to sound and rhythm. The text he has prepared for the composer is sure to avoid the monotony of what could be the too regular beat of the French language. The length of lines again varies enormously: besides the ordinary lines of twelve, ten, eight and six syllables, there are frequent occurrences of lines of five, four and even three syllables. The Passover scene contains a stanza:

> O coupable trame!
> O forfait infâme!
> Au fond de mon âme
> Je tremble et frémis!
> Et de sa tendresse
> L'innocent ivresse
> M'accable et oppresse
> D'un nouveau mépris![9]

This is perhaps not great poetry. Yet it is perfectly suited to the needs of the composer: the musicality of the short lines, composed of an uneven number of syllables, and the rhymes occurring at frequent intervals, creates a definite musicality of the line. The effect is heightened by the rhyme scheme of *aaabcccb*. The final vowels of *a* and *c* are long and sustained; the final vowels of *b* are short and clipped.

These linguistic exercises abound in the text, and reach their height perhaps in an amazing series of three-syllable lines. French lends itself to rhyme much more than English does, so that the effect of such an accumulation of rhymes is musical rather than oppressive:

> Non, non, Dieu m'éclaire!
> fille chère,
> Près d'un père
> Viens mourir;
> Et pardonne,
> Quand il donne
> La couronne
> Du martyre.[10]

This stanza continues in the same form for another eight lines.

Once again Scribe has given the composer all he could ask for in fulfilling the theoretical requirements of an opera: the combination of music, art (costumes and decor), literature and dance (the wine fountain scene and the banquet). It is no wonder that the result was one of the most successful of all French operas of the nineteenth century.

IX   Les Huguenots

On February 29, 1836, was produced what was to become one of the most famous and influential operas in the history of music. *The Huguenots*, with music by Meyerbeer, was instrumental in effecting a veritable revolution in operatic music.

The subject is an awesome one: the St. Bartholomew's day massacre. This, the most infamous event in the long history of religious disturbances occurred in France, when, in 1572, the Catholics literally massacred every Protestant to be found in Paris. The following dawn broke over a city from which the Protestant Huguenot element had quite simply been eliminated.

The revolution caused in the musical world by the opera is, of course, a consequence of the innovations of the score. However, it would be incorrect to reject the libretto as without influence in this revolution. Many reasons seem to suggest the importance of the text in determining the direction which Meyerbeer was to take.

Music critics recognize a clear distinction between Meyerbeer's earlier "Italian" operas and his French operas. In *Huguenots*, the first of the French operas, it is only logical to see Scribe's text as an important influence in creating the new manner.

The subject, a serious one, is a basic struggle between the two religions, a subject Scribe had already taken up with great effect in *La Juive*, presented the previous year, where the conflict is between Christians and Jews. *Huguenots*, however, has the added dramatic advantage of being tied closely to an historic event, the Massacre, which holds great potential emotion for every French listener.

The subject parallels contemporary theater and the novel. Hugo had been developing the tenets of the historical drama since his experiments with *Cromwell* in 1826. And indeed, Vigny wrote a novel, *Chronicles of the Times of Charles IX* (1829), based on the St. Bartholomew's day massacre. As early as 1802, Chateaubriand, in his *Genius of Christianity*, had advocated the use of Christian themes for literary development, as being far more capable of moving the public than the old classical themes.

There is at least as great an opposition between the opera of Meyerbeer and those that had gone before as there was between the new theatrical form of the *drame* and the old classical tragedies. Opera had heretofore depended to a large extent on classical mythological themes. At its inception, opera, as a combination of all the arts, was looked upon as an ideal, something belonging to another world, and thus not directly attached to the world of reality. Even Rossini in his serious operas, depends to a great extent on such themes: *Tancredi, Armida,* and so on. Even his historical works such as *Elizabeth, Queen of England, William Tell* and the like, are not intimately tied to the history of the public's own country. One is tempted to recall Diderot's assessment of Richardson when he declared that the Englishman's novels constituted a new genre, quite distinct from the former frivolous novels, in that they were *serious.*

Nothing could be more serious than the background of *Huguenots.* Against this background is projected a pathetic individual history that complements the national tragedy. The opera opens with a dinner hosted by the Count de Nevers. Dinner waits for a late arrival: Raoul de Nangis, a Huguenot and outsider, admitted through the protection of the Huguenot leader, Admiral de Colligny. A mysterious woman arrives. The guests all assume that she is the most recent of the Count's mistresses. Raoul is horrified when he recognizes her as the unknown young lady he had earlier rescued from a mob. He had immediately fallen in love with her, and the passion was reciprocated. Actually, this is Valentine, who had been promised by her father to Nevers. She is here to ask the marriage be abandoned, since she is now in love. Always the consummate gentleman, Nevers agrees, although reluctantly.

Meanwhile, Marguerite de Navarre, Queen of Navarre and sister to the King of France, Charles IX, sends a letter to Raoul asking him to come to her. She intends to arrange a marriage between Raoul and Valentine, since she knows of their encounter, and further, is anxious to heal the wounds of Catholics and Protestants by uniting the Huguenot Raoul to the Catholic Valentine. Those attending the Count's dinner recognize the hand and seal of the Queen, and immediately assume that the Queen has fallen in love with Raoul. At once their attitude changes from the rather diffident attitude they had first shown; they now fawn abjectly over Raoul, expecting him to be the new favorite.

Raoul goes to meet the Queen. She dazzles the young man—and is, in turn, on the point of becoming emotionally involved herself—but she holds back. When the courtiers arrive, she announces her plans for the marriage, but Raoul refuses, still believing Valentine had deceived him. A duel is prevented for the moment, since the courtiers have been called to Paris; but later when the scene shifts to Paris, Raoul announces he is ready. Saint-Bris, Valentine's father, is ready to fight a duel to avenge the insult to his daughter; but his friends, claiming the rules of honor do not apply when one is dealing with Huguenots, arrange to lie in ambush for Raoul. Raoul is on the point of being killed when the Huguenot sympathisers are roused and rescue Raoul with his friends.

It is learned that, under protest, Valentine has married Nevers. She still loves Raoul, however, and had attempted to warn him of the ambush, but in vain. Raoul comes to see Valentine at her father's mansion, braving death. There he learns of the plotted massacre of the Protestants. He wishes to warn them, but the signal sounds before he can carry out his plan. Meanwhile, Valentine has confessed her love for him, although she is still loyal to her husband, particularly because he has broken his sword rather than take part in the massacre.

The scene shifts to the Hôtel de Nesle, where Marguerite and the Protestant sympathisers are gathered. Raoul, covered with blood, rushes in to announce the massacre. The scene shifts to a church, where the few remaining Huguenots are clustered seeking sanctuary. Raoul and Valentine meet there. The church proves to be no sanctuary, however, as the Catholics break down the portals and massacre the innocents. Raoul is injured, and he and Valentine rush out into the street and collapse. In the final scene, in the street, a group of marauding Catholics arrive. They demand to know whether Raoul and Valentine are Catholics. Raoul bravely proclaims himself a Huguenot. Valentine does the same. They are shot by the group led by Saint-Bris, who only too late recognizes that he has killed his own daughter.

A good deal of Scribe's theatrical technique comes into the making of the libretto. The device of mistaking one person for another is an important one; the action would not develop as it does without Raoul's having mistaken Valentine for one of the Count's mistresses. Likewise, the trick of having a letter sent by the Queen to Raoul, acting as an intermediary between him and Valentine, suggests the similar technique which Scribe was to use in *Adrienne Lecouvreur* some years later, when la Duclos is used by the Princess de Bouillon to write her love notes to Maurice de Saxe, with the result that the Prince de Bouillon thinks that la Duclos has deserted him for Maurice. Finally, there are many touches of the *pièce bien faite* dear to Scribe: little elements of preparation and construction which serve to motivate the action and render it cohesive. One can cite such examples as the mention of Admiral de Colligny as Raoul's protector early in the play, which keeps the character in mind for the end of the opera when reference is made to the killing of the Admiral in the course of the massacre. In a similar way, given Nevers's reputation as a womaniser and profligate (he leads a chorus at the beginning of the opera, indicating his wish to convert Raoul to the true gods "of pleasure and love"—a particularly strong statement in view of the deeply religious tone of the plot) it is difficult to see him as the honorable man of the final scenes, refusing to take part in the massacre. However, we have been prepared for this side of his character already in the first act by his acceptance of Valentine's request not to marry him.

If the opera is not frequently presented today, the reasons are easy to understand. It is in five acts, the fifth act consisting of three scenes. Each one of these has its own elaborate setting. Two of the scenes involve pitched battles with hordes of singers and actors. Finally the music requires an exceptional tenor, an exceptional mezzo, and two exceptional sopranos. The music is at many points excessively difficult for the singer, although very rewarding to the audience. The cost of a worthy production of the opera would certainly go beyond the capacity of most modern opera houses.

Huguenots emphasizes once again the subservience of the words to the music. All shadings of literary meaning, any nuance of psychology, must be lost, as there is a preponderance of concerted singing in which everyone is singing on a different subject. Moreover, the way Meyerbeer sets the words in this opera is frequently indicative of the lack of interest in producing an understandable sung text: frequently (as with the drinking chorus of the first act) the rhythm of the French language is distorted to the point of being unrecognizable on the level of language. Instead, Meyerbeer has taken the broad sweep of the action and extracted the basic emotion from it. It is this emotion which he transmits to his listeners. When, in several scenes of disorder, the Lutheran hymn "Ein' feste Burg ist unsere Gott" soars over the other music, the emotional effect is incomparable.

X   Le Prophète

Again, in collaboration with Meyerbeer, Scribe produced another of the most influential of operas to come out of the French nineteenth century: *Le Prophète*, premiered on April 16, 1849. The story, in typical Scribe fashion, is rather loosely based on history, with alterations of the facts to suit the dramatic purposes.

The story takes place in sixteenth-century Holland, and is constructed around the incidents involved in the Anabaptist uprising under the leadership of the "prophet" John of Leyden. The action of the opera begins with John's mother, Fidès, coming to Dordrecht to convey to Berthe her son's proposal of marriage. However, Berthe cannot leave to marry John without the permission of the feudal overlord, Oberthal. Rather capriciously he refuses this permission and has Berthe taken to his castle. Meanwhile, three Anabaptists have appeared in Dordrecht to preach their uprising, which is a curious combination of religious fervor, political revolutionary sentiment directed at the overthrow of the feudal lords, and a base kind of venality seeking for personal gain.

The second act is in Leyden, in the inn of Fidès, where John is awaiting the outcome of his mother's mission to Dordrecht. The Anabaptists who have put in an appearance here, too, are struck by the resemblance between John and the representation of David in a miraculous portrait that hangs in the Muenster cathedral. They decide that he is the promised Messiah who will lead their battles. At first John is deaf to their suggestions, but when, upon the return of Fidès he learns of Oberthal's refusal, he decides to lead the Anabaptists as a means of wreaking vengeance on Oberthal.

To enhance his credibility as the prophet, the Anabaptists insist that he leave his mother—and we learn later that he has been represented to Fidès as having been killed. Thus neither she nor Berthe knows the identity of the Prophet.

The forces of the Anabaptists are gathered before Muenster, preparing for the final assault. They falter, fearing for a moment defeat, and are even on the point of denying John, when his mystical presence serves to revitalize them. They enter the city triumphant.

As preparations are being made for the coronation of John, Fidès appears in Muenster, still thinking her son dead. She enters the cathedral where she sees John and recognizes him. However, he dares not recognize her, as the Anabaptists have sworn to kill her if he does so. Their fear is understandable: for a moment, the people believe Fidès when she claims John her son, and in that moment they turn away from him as a false prophet and not the Son of God. Again John mesmerises the populace and the ceremonies continue.

Later, John comes to Fidès to ask forgiveness. For a long time it is impossible for Fidès to give this absolution: the Prophet's crimes have been too great, in both the temporal and spiritual realm. He has caused death and carnage throughout Germany, and he has claimed to be the Son of God. Maternal love finally wins out, however; she gives her forgiveness, and brings John to a realization of his guilt.

Berthe appears. She had jumped from the battlements of Oberthal's castle into the water, expecting to die. But she has been saved, and has made her way to Muenster where she has a relative who is an intimate of the castle. She is thus able to find her way to Fidès. She tells of stores of saltpeter in the crypt, and indicates her intention of destroying the castle. However, when she recognizes John as the Prophet, she is so horrified that she stabs herself on the spot.

News arrives that Oberthal and the forces of the Emperor are arriving to destroy John. John decides on punishment for himself and the others: when the Anabaptists are inside the chamber, he has the doors closed and ignites the saltpeter. A great detonation is set off, destroying the castle and all within it.

Once again the materials offered by the librettist to the composer are full of potential. The libretto is studded with strong expressions of passions of various kinds, ideally suited for musical transmission. At the very beginning Berthe is expressing her love for John. In Act II, John gives vent to his emotions in a powerful scene where Berthe has escaped from Oberthal and is being hidden by John. Oberthal brings forth Fidès and threatens to kill her if John does not deliver Berthe.

Fidès also has ample opportunity for expressing her emotions, whether they be her maternal feelings toward her son or her state of abject poverty and misery combined with physical exhaustion upon her arrival in Muenster.

The requirements of spectacle are likewise amply provided for. The great scene of the coronation is filled with magnificent visual possibilities: Scribe describes the coronation procession in detail. The vast nave of the cathedral is an ideal setting for this. Again, the final scene of destruction is easily the equal of other famous scenes of similar nature: one thinks immediately of the destruction of the temple which Saint-Saens was to depict at the end of *Samson and Delilah*.

It is no coincidence that the Coronation March inspired by this scene has remained the most consistently popular piece in the opera, having became a frequent concert number.

XI   The Bloody Nun

Scribe's only collaboration with Charles Gounod, the celebrated composer of *Faust* and *Romeo and Juliet*, was *La Nonne sanglante* of 1854. The author did not originally write the text for Gounod. In turn he offered it to Meyerbeer and Berlioz. Meyerbeer appears not to have been enthusiastic over the text, and with Berlioz, although he began work on the score,[11] contractual agreements prevented its acceptance by the Paris Opera, and so Scribe withdrew the libretto from Berlioz and confided it to Gounod.

The story comes from an episode in Matthew Gregory Lewis's famed Gothic novel, *The Monk*. The basic lines of the Bloody Nun episode are identical in Lewis and the opera: a young man loves Agnes, but is not allowed to marry her. They decide to have her impersonate the Nun, a well-known spectre of the castle. The veiled figure appears, and they depart together. But the figure actually is the Nun, and from that moment he is haunted, until she is exorcised, thus allowing the marriage of the two young people.

What Scribe does to this source material shows what indeed a well-made play is made of, or—in this case, a well-made opera. He introduces a great many details which alter the story and make it more dramatic and more cohesive. Rodolphe cannot marry Agnes because she has been promised to his brother. When he departs with the Nun, instead of her disappearing after a carriage accident, she accompanies Rodolphe to the ancient castle of his ancestors, now in ruins. Under her influence, the castle is magically restored to its former splendor and peopled by a host of ghosts, including Rodolphe's brother (we later learn that he has just been killed in battle.)

The Nun reveals to Rodolphe that she was murdered and cannot rest until her murderer is killed. To rid himself of the apparition, Rodolphe promises to kill the murderer, who will be revealed to him by the appearance of a bloody cross on his breast.

Meanwhile Rodolphe's page arrives to report that with the death of the brother the family is now anxious to have Rodolphe marry Agnes. They return to the castle, but he discovers that the murderer he must kill is his own father. This is again the typical Scribean dilemma: he must kill his father or lose the woman he loves. He cannot commit the murder, however, and departs. This rekindles the battles between the families of Agnes and Rodolphe which the marriage was supposed to end.

In the final scene, the father is at the tomb of the Nun. He begs to be allowed to expiate his crime. Some of the opposition party pass; they have learned that Rodolphe is to enter the chapel, where they intend to assassinate him. The father himself goes to the chapel so that he will be killed instead of Rodolphe. The Nun accepts this sacrifice and releases Rodolphe.

In the Lewis novel, all that was needed to exorcise the Nun was to bury her bones which had been left in a cave without sepulture, which revelation is made to the hero by a mysterious individual at an inn.

The story, as transformed by Scribe, is considerably more cohesive and, through the added conflicts he puts into his work involves the spectator to a much greater degree.

There are the other elements typical of the opera: the grandiose setting, the ballet of villagers, the drinking song. Of these, it is certainly the decor which strikes us as the most ambitious and most original. The scene at the ruined castle is described in detail. The execution must have been very difficult, but again, the solving of vast problems of setting and decoration traditionally forms one of the delights of opera. Here is how Scribe describes the scene:

The ruins of a Gothic castle. A vast hall whose windows and porticos are half destroyed. In the middle of the stage, the remains of a great stone table and chairs covered with ivy and wild plants. The moon lights this scene and reveals in the distance at the top of a mountain a hermitage.

Then comes the transformation:

The moon disappears. The porticos and windows which were in ruins regain their original form and elegance. The remains of the stone table change into a vast table covered with richly served foods. All around, numerous seats. The torches which cover the table ignite suddenly, as well as the candelabra lighting the hall, and in place of the darkness, the brilliance of light on the gilded wood and the groups of arms glistening all round. All this change has taken place in silence.[12]

The descriptions of the sepulchral guests, pale of face and gliding rather than walking across the stage, add to the effect of the scene. Scribe has certainly not forgotten, in this opera, the precepts which guided him in the writing of his plays. But at the same time, he was acutely aware of the elements which would prove effective in an operatic setting.

XII   *Italian Operas*

Scribe's only direct collaboration with Verdi was with *Les Vêpres siciliennes*. There was a kind of collaboration later in that Scribe's play *Le Bal masqué* was transformed into the libretto for *Un ballo in maschera;* but in that case Scribe was not to take part in the actual writing of the libretto. The collaboration on the *Vespers*, however, is nonetheless significant.

It is important to remember that at the time Verdi was no beginner. He already had behind him *Rigoletto, Traviata* and *Trovatore*, and, despite some problems with public reaction, was still a reigning composer for the opera. The fact that he could no doubt have had any collaborator he wished and yet chose Scribe, seems to indicate that Verdi considered him the best choice, particularly for a French opera.

The Paris Opera had commissioned the work from Verdi. Much as Donizetti relied on Scribe for pleasing the intricacies of French taste, Verdi seemed ready to do likewise. The dictated French form, five acts and the obligatory ballet, are the obvious elements of the French orientation. Parenthetically, it may be useful to suggest that, despite the moaning of critics over Verdi's necessity of bending to the French taste, we may well be much the better for it. Some of the most interesting music in the opera is in the ballet—a very French ballet—and we would certainly be the poorer without it. As is so frequently the case, the ballet is dramatically hard to justify: the Sicilian conspiracy is afoot, but all stops dead for thirty minutes while we are treated to a depiction of the four seasons danced by ballerinas appropriately costumed in icicles and greenery.

But to offer objections on this nondramatic ground is again to misunderstand the function of opera. Certainly such an interruption in a classical tragedy would be entirely out of place. These objections are particularly understandable in cases such as the ballet in Gounod's *Romeo and Juliet* where Juliet takes the supposed poison, then starts to "die," only to be interrupted by a prolonged ballet. Once the ballet is finished, the action is allowed to continue. For Anglo-Saxon audiences at least, the model of Shakespeare's play is too present in the mind to allow easy acceptance of such a device. (Berlioz is much more successful in his *Romeo and Juliet* when limiting the ballet to the earlier—too early for convention—ballets of the Capulet reception scene.)

Once again, however, the author whose purpose dictates the effects of a classical tragedy, writes a classical tragedy and not an opera. The operatic genre not only permits, but encourages, such interruptions as adding to the overall cumulative effect of music, dance, literature and painting. Suffice it to repeat that some of the most interesting music of the opera occurs in the ballet.

The "Sicilian Vespers" refer to a Sicilian uprising against the French occupying forces in 1282, the revolt led by Giovanni da Procida. As Scribe prepares the scenario, we are involved on a personal rather than national level, and merely witness the flurries of the approaching doom as background to the individual action. The Vespers themselves do not really figure in the opera: the massacre begins only as the final curtain is falling. The event serves more as a menacing cloud, ever hovering over the action taking place among the principals.

This action is centered around Arrigo, who is the long-lost son of Monforte, leader of the French occupiers. The object of Arrigo's affections is Elena, whose brother has perished at the hands of the French. Monforte, however, not pictured as a tyrant, displays great generosity, in the first instance in accepting Arrigo's liberation at the hands of the courts after an accusation of treason. Soon Giovanni da Procida arrives. He is the mastermind behind the massacre being planned. Arrigo later is asked, then forced, to go to the palace to attend a feast, which will become the excuse for the extended ballet. Monforte has learned the identity of Arrigo: the mother had sought vengeance by raising their son in ignorance of his birth and in hatred for Monforte. When Monforte tells Arrigo the story of his birth, Arrigo is placed in the typical Scribean dilemma: if he abandons the conspiracy he is dishonorable; if he denies his father he is dishonorable. For the time being he denies his father. But at the moment when Elena rushes up to kill Monforte, Arrigo interposes himself to save his father. Elena, taken off to prison, turns against Arrigo. But when he visits her, he explains the circumstances and all is forgiven. Monforte again shows his clemency by offering to liberate Elena if Arrigo will acknowledge his parenthood. Again Arrigo refuses, but carried away by emotion, he calls Monforte, "father." Elena is freed and there is no longer any impediment to their marriage. The festivities are prepared, but at the last moment we learn that Procida has planned to use the sounding of the marriage bells to signal the beginning of the uprising. A final Scribean dilemma: Elena will be signalling the start of the massacre if she goes ahead with the marriage she so ardently desires. She chooses to give up the marriage, but Monforte insists on carrying it out. The bells ring and the massacre begins.

The story of the Sicilian Vespers, although not having the currency that was to be found in the massacre of St. Bartholomew's day, was still a well-known event. It was known through history but also through literature. A few years earlier, in particular, one of the most successful of popular novelists, Lamothe-Langon, had been very successful with a novel on the Vespers entitled simply *Jean de Procida*. The even better-known dramatist, Casimir Delavigne, had also written a play on the subject—a tragedy, *Les Vêpres siciliennes*. Many critics have complained of Scribe's handling of the subject, citing in particular the romanesque circumstances and events—the all-too-frequent coincidences. However, it must not be forgotten that in spite of the *philosophes* of the eighteenth century, in conservative circles (an opera belongs certainly to conservative circles), there was explicit faith in providence. The hand of providence making itself felt in a work of literature was not, therefore, something unbelievable, but the most natural of events.

Some of the contemporary critics (such as the composer Berlioz) hailed the opera as a perfect mixture of French and Italian influences. It is suggested that the French influences played a large role in the developing of Verdi's final manner as illustrated by *Falstaff*.

When it is played today, the opera is invariably given in an Italian version. At times, in following the score, one can sense the French intonations in the music behind the Italian words, which do not form an ideal accompaniment to the music. Perhaps this is the reason the opera has not enjoyed greater success in modern times.

Modern performances, however, are by no means rare. Certainly, Verdi, who had already achieved mastery in his previous operas, was showing no signs of decadence here. There is a long history of the disputes between Verdi and Scribe over the libretto of this opera. To take them at face value, the collaboration would seem to have been doomed to failure. It is far more likely, however, that the seriousness of the disputes should be heavily discounted. We have two artistic temperaments engaged with one another, and it is rare under such circumstances that all should run smoothly. On balance, it would appear that Scribe once again supplied the composer with a close-to-ideal vehicle for the projected music. The required ballets and banquet scenes, the large crowds with their homely merriment, the impending doom of the massacre, all contribute to the desired effect. Perhaps the collaboration was not ideal to the extent that Verdi's collaborations with Italian librettists were, but it is doubtful that any other French librettist could have surpassed Scribe.

XIII L'Africaine

Scribe's last libretto was another collaboration with Meyerbeer: *L'Africaine*, which was not to be produced until April 28, 1865, after the librettist's death. Meyerbeer was said to have preferred this opera to all his others, but in terms of presentation, *Les Huguenots* has probably proven to be more popular. The aria (best known by its Italian title) "O Paradiso," from the fourth act, and the "Sleeping Song" from Act II are some of the most popular of opera arias. The latest recorded interpreter of the Act II aria is Leontyne Price. "O Paradiso" has been sung by almost every tenor from Caruso to Mario Lanza.

Again, we have the typical five-act format traditional in the French Grand Opera of the time. The opening of Act IV, on the island, provides the appropriate opportunity for the required ballet.

The opera begins at the moment when news arrives in Lisbon of the shipwreck of Bernard Díaz and the loss of all hands. Inès is particularly upset, since she is in love with Vasco da Gama who had accompanied Diaz. She is soon consoled, however, when Vasco appears, having escaped the disaster and bringing back charts of the route to the Indies around the Cape of Good Hope. He also brings back two slaves to prove his contention that new lands were to be found beyond the African cape.

Meanwhile, the father of Inès orders his daughter to marry an important member of the court, Don Pedro. Vasco appears as a rival to him, so Pedro arranges to have the Council declare that Vasco's plans for a return voyage to find the safe passage around the Cape are an insane undertaking. Vasco is so incensed that he insults the Council, and the Grand Inquisitor declares him a heretic for maintaining that there exist new lands not mentioned in the Bible. Vasco and his two slaves are sent to prison. The female slave, Sélika, loves Vasco and prevents the male slave, Nélusko, from killing him. We learn that Sélika is actually Queen of her land, which is apparently Madagascar, although the descriptive elements are much more reminiscent of India.

In order to free Vasco, Inès has married Don Pedro, who has had himself named chief of the new expedition to the Cape. He takes along the two slaves; Nélusko secretly rejoices, intending to lead the expedition to disaster.

The third act takes place on board Don Pedro's ship as it approaches the Cape. A ship in the distance seems to be leading them, but Nélusko convinces Don Pedro he must change course. When they do this, the other ship comes alongside; it is Vasco da Gama who, liberated from prison, has liquidated all his possessions in order to charter a ship to return to the Cape. Faster than Don Pedro's ship, he has already found the safe passage around the Cape. He warns Don Pedro that they are headed for the same reef on which Bernard Díaz had foundered. Don Pedro will not listen, and the ship goes aground, to be immediately boarded by natives intent on massacring the Portuguese. Nélusko gloats.

Vasco, however, has escaped the shipwreck and massacre and reached land. Sélika protects him from being killed by claiming he is her husband. But it appears Inès also has escaped the holocaust. Vasco realizes that he still loves her, and Sélika is quick to realize this too. In a gesture of generosity, she allows Vasco and Inès to escape from the island in order to return to Portugal. Sélika and Nélusko, watching their ship depart, take poison.

Again, Scribe has prepared a libretto loosely based on history, but using the history only as a background against which the less cosmic events are projected. Vasco da Gama is known to everyone, just as the Sicilian Vespers and the St. Bartholomew's day massacre were part of each spectator's historical baggage. By a kind of osmosis, his characters take on a historical coloring that suits well the purposes of the composer.

XIV   *Opera as a Genre*

Opera subject matter tends to be conservative. Indeed, much of *L'Africaine* reminds us of earlier developments on the literary scene. The type of historical drama represented by the opera's libretto is very close to the type of drama being written by Victor Hugo at the beginning of the nineteenth century, almost forty years earlier. Even more striking, the local color and exoticism represented by the Malagasy natives and scenery are entirely reminiscent of Bernardin de Saint-Pierre's exotic novel of an island in the Indian Ocean, *Paul and Virginia*, which dates from a hundred years before the presentation of the opera.

Such traditionalism is the rule rather than the exception in opera. And yet, at the same time that we see this extreme conservatism in the subject matter, we find significant innovation in various areas. Exotic music was going to become extremely important in opera: Spanish, Chinese, Japanese tonalities were going to be heard. But in Meyerbeer's treatment of Malagasy exoticism we find the techniques at their outset.

There is yet another extremely interesting innovation to be found in the opera, due entirely to Scribe's libretto. Act Three takes place on shipboard, but we do not see merely the top deck of the ship. Scribe's instructions indicate that the audience is to see a cross-section of the ship, with the upper deck on top, but the second deck visible below. This in turn is divided into two sections. On deck are the praying sailors; below, in one section are Inès and her attendants, including Sélika. The other section is Don Pedro's cabin. Characters move from one setting to another in the course of the act. This simultaneous stage setting not only recalls the experiments in simultaneous settings and simultaneous action which were presented by Marinetti and his futurist school in Paris in the 1920s, but even antedates the scenic innovations of Gordon Craig and Adolph Appia at the end of the nineteenth century. The technique is still modern today. The twentieth-century equivalent, the split-screen technique in films and television is a recent innovation and still retains its novelty for today's spectator.

What then can be said of Scribe's entire career of musical involvement? Certainly we are dealing with the same man who was the author of the plays; the same considerations of structure and elaboration are present in both plays and operas. The same attention to preparation of events occurs in the libretti as in the dramas.

The musical genre, however, has its own rules and its own needs. The failure to recognize this fact is what has led to the critics' parrot-like repetition of their claims that Scribe as a librettist was mediocre and insignificant. The words of an opera, taken out of the musical context, will almost invariably be adjudged silly and valueless. The conventions must be accepted. All the other conventions should be easily accepted after the overwhelming convention of having the principals sing rather than speak.

Scribe gave great attention then, first of all to a careful structure in which events were motivated and explained. But in addition he was entirely aware of the requirements of opera. This almost necessarily meant a choice of subject matters far different from those he chose for the dramatic plays. The common, everyday situations, placed in commonplace settings, were hardly the right subject matter for grand opera. His works for the opera house needed to supply the composer with ample opportunity for painting broad canvasses of raw emotion, avoiding the shadings of spoken drama. There needed to be room for ample exercise of the other arts, dance and painting, in order for the spectacle to be complete.

Opera is, of course, quite artificial, and the conventions which must be accepted are numerous. But the acceptance of these conventions produces an art form which is perhaps the most effective art form, if judged by the effect it has on its audience. One has merely to witness the reactions of an opera audience compared to those of a conventional drama. The mass reaction which is part of the theatrical experience is carried in opera to an almost unbelievable level. A few polite curtain calls may end a drama, while the opera evokes paroxysms of voiced emotion from the audience.

As the very particular effect of a classical tragedy can be created only through the observance of the rules, the conventions of that genre, in opera, the combination of all the arts, as the eighteenth century saw it, can create an experience which is unlike any other in the intensity of the reaction on the part of the audience.

CHAPTER 7

Conclusion

TO what conclusions does a reexamination of Scribe lead us?
First, the reexamination is self-justifying in that the existing
body of criticism does not do justice to the playwright. He was attacked from all sides, by critics who demanded a more "literary" expression, by fellow authors who were jealous of his success. Only the
public liked Scribe, the public and perhaps also the directors and
the opera composers who obviously prized his work. Scribe could
always be counted on to bring in the cash receipts.

The anecdote has been recounted about Scribe and the plaque on
his house thanking the public for having paid so many admissions to
his plays that he was able to afford such a grand place. Somehow,
the success of an author in the commercial area is to be frowned upon; it is demeaning to earn money from the public. Indeed, if one is
a public success, by some Flaubertian scorn of the bourgeoisie, such
a success must be considered a condemnation.

There are certainly many examples of the established literary
figures who could not achieve popular success. Gerard de Nerval,
who, according to the anecdote, committed suicide in desperation
at Scribe's success, had attempted a career as a playwright. His most
ambitious dramatic effort, a play called *Léo Burkhardt* certainly
received no measure of success. The same can be said of his opera
libretto, *Les Monténégrins.* The little success he had dramatically
was in collaboration with Dumas. It was indeed a severe blow to discover one can have success only in collaboration with another
author.

Stendhal, too, had dramatic ambitions. His early years in Paris
were devoted to the study of philosophy and physiology in order to
make himself into a great playwright. All he managed to produce
were some fragments that indicate we are fortunate that Stendhal

154

abandoned the theater. But even his novels can hardly be said to have been crowned with success during his lifetime. He was quite aware of his limited appeal, hence his dedication "To the Happy Few." Flaubert, of course, made no bones about ignoring popular reaction. Whatever was popularly acceptable was obviously mediocre, according to his thinking. Villiers de l'Isle-Adam wanted to write dramas as well. Plays such as *Axël* may be admired by critics, but they are scarcely playable.

It is necessary, therefore, to push aside not only the criticisms of the envious, but also the criticisms of the well-intentioned "literary" critics. For these, raised in the school of classical drama, the approximation of common everyday spoken language that Scribe gives us is anathema. In spite of the Romantic revolution, much of the drama of the nineteenth century still bore the weight of the older works. Victor Hugo in his *Hernani* and *Ruy Blas* still has his characters speaking in alexandrine verses, albeit with an occasional enjambment or vagary of verse to shake up the complacent. Dumas père, although using prose for his characters, scarcely uses what we would term natural languages in his romantic plays, whether they be historical, as in *Henri III and his Court*, or sentimental, as in *Antony*. Such authors were convinced that too close an imitation of nature would depart from the world of art. Scribe, by his language, as in so many other ways, was able to take the most commonplace elements and turn them into a play capable of captivating an audience.

Besides his attention to the commonplace in language, he was equally capable of exploiting the commonplace in life. Rarely is one of Scribe's situations, at least outside the operas, by any means exceptional. Here again the aesthete might claim that such vile and subservient imitation of nature could not be worthy of a work of art. After all, these critics had behind them the full force of eighteenth-century thought, which dictated that not all of nature is appropriate for art; the artist of good taste must choose "beautiful nature" out of the great mass of nature, to utilize in his art.

A simple comparison of Hugo and Scribe shows to what extent the concepts differ. In *Ruy Blas* a bandit loves a Queen. Everything is on a heroic level, and the characters act accordingly. Even when Scribe portrays Queens and Duchesses, as in *The Glass of Water*, their motivations and their reactions are those of any ordinary person.

The concept of the well-made play is a constant refrain in connection with Scribe. The immediate question always comes to mind: who would want to write a poorly-made play? But somehow the "literary" authors and critics seem to consider too close an attention to form as another element debasing art. Perhaps this comes from the historic dichotomy between authors and actors in France.

Because they were considered to lead highly immoral lives, actors were historically on the fringe of French society. Racine could write for the theater, remaining at a distance, without sullying his honor. But Molière, a man of the theater, an actor, lost all social status. Indeed, an actor, immediately he set foot on the stage, was automatically excommunicated. Molière, on his death, was refused Christian burial because of his theatrical affiliations.

Perhaps as a result of this public sentiment, many authors felt themselves separate from the workings of the theater. Scribe, who was intimately involved in all aspects of his plays, was once again impure.

But his popular success shows that his technique was an able one. He knew how to choose a good situation, he developed the appropriate characters, and he resolved his actions with almost unparalleled skill. His endings are not necessarily surprises, since we can usually guess what the end result will be. Scribe's talent is in the ingenuity with which he brings about the desired end, an ingenuity which has nothing of the contrived about it, quite the contrary. Scribe is able to order his actions to the point that his chosen ending is an absolute necessity, given the train of events he has portrayed.

Certainly the fame of Scribe and his plays has spread throughout the world. He is, perhaps for the moment, under an eclipse, in spite of some indications of a revival (the Comédie Française revival of *The Glass of Water,* for example). But the material is there for a complete rehabilitation of Scribe, a rehabilitation similar to that which occurred with Feydeau, who thirty years ago was one of the most forgotten of recent dramatists, but who is now the subject of countless revivals. The lack of the tradition of the repertory theater in America is a hindrance to such a rehabilitation; but in France and England, where the tradition is a strong one, Feydeau is already firmly established, so perhaps Scribe will not be far behind. His enormous contribution to the various modes of theatrical presentation and his effect upon the history of the theater indicate his importance, while the quality of his work deserves a place in the living theater of today.

Notes and References

Chapter One

1. Some sources give December 25, as the date of his birth, but in an unpublished letter Scribe himself gives his birth date as December 24. The name of the Rue Trousse-Vache was changed to Rue de la Régnie in 1822.

2. Vincent-Antoine Arnault (1766 - 1834) wrote tragedies. A follower of Napoleon, he was exiled in 1816 but allowed to return to France in 1819. In 1829 he was elected to the Académie Française.

3. General Jean-Victor Moreau (1763 - 1813) had a brilliant career in the republican army. In 1804, after he had retired, a group of conspirators, headed by Bernadotte, planned to overthrow Napoleon. Moreau refused to assist them, but did not reveal the plot to Napoleon either, and after it had failed, he was tried for treason. Bonnet was appointed to defend him, and the trial had many political overtones; his antagonist was Napoleon. Despite the pressure, Bonnet gained exile rather than death for Moreau. The "victory" was famous throughout France.

4. Sources vary, but he seems to have had an annual income of between three and five thousand francs.

5. Loménie, *Galerie des contemporains illustres*, v. 3 (Paris: A. René. n.d.), p. 21.

6. "Scribe" *Grand Dictionnaire universel du XIXe Siècle*, ed. Pierre Larousse (Paris: Administration du Grand Dictionnaire universel, 1875).

7. Marcel Charlot, *Théâtre choisi d'Eugène Scribe* (Paris: Librairie Delagrave, 1923), p. 22.

8. The complete story, with details is contained in Théodore Muret's *L'Histoire par le théâtre 1789 - 1851* (Paris: Amyot, 1865), pp. 198 - 230.

9. Eugène Mirecourt, *Scribe* (Paris: J.-P. Roret, 1854), p. 82.

10. *The North American Review* (October, 1863), p. 332.

11. Brander Matthews, *French Dramatists of the Nineteenth Century* (New York: Scribner's, 1881), p. 87.

12. Mirecourt, pp. 66 - 67n.

13. Mirecourt, pp. 42 - 43.

14. *Grand Dictionnaire universel.*

15. Mirecourt, pp. 69 - 70.

16. Mirecourt, pp. 71 - 73.

17. Grand Dictionnaire Universel.

18. *Foyer du Gymnase* (Prologue with Mélesville and Bayard) and *Une faute*, written alone. Both opened August 12.

19. Mirecourt, pp. 52 - 54.

20. Mirecourt, pp. 54 - 56.

21. Act IV. Quoted in Théodore de Banville, *Mes Souvenirs* (Paris: G. Charpentier, 1882), pp. 345ff.

22. Loménie, pp. 18 - 19.

23. Count Johann Friedrich von Struensée (1737 - 1772) was a German doctor and statesman who, by controlling Christian VII, ruled Denmark from 1770 to 1772. Although he initiated such reforms as freedom of the press, he was overthrown by the Dowager Queen Juliana Maria and her party. Charged with being the Queen's lover, he confessed and was executed April 25, 1772.

24. Matthews, p. 86.

25. J. Rolland, *Les Comédies historiques et politiques d'Eugène Scribe* (Paris: Bibliothèque des Hautes-Etudes Sociales, 1933) p. 39.

26. Matthews, p. 88.

27. *Grand Dictionnaire universel.*

28. Eugène Scribe, *Oeuvres complètes* (Paris: Dentu, 1874), I, 20.

29. Scribe, I, 32.

30. The printed edition lists his co-author as "Thérèse Essler," but the *Grand Dictionnaire universel* identifies her as Fanny Ellsler.

31. Mirecourt, pp. 76 - 77. He gives the title of the play as *Camélias* and says it could not be done because Dumas fils' *La Dame aux camélias* had just appeared. This would put the date at 1852. Scribe, however, had written *Camilla* in 1832, and Mirecourt may be in error.

32. Françisque Sarcey, *Quarante ans de théâtre* (Paris: Bibliothéque des Annales politiques et littéraires, 1900 - 1902), IV, 116.

33. Sarcey, IV, 148 - 54.

34. *North American Review*, p. 335.

35. Mirecourt, p. 75.

36. According to history, Maurice de Saxe, in order to regain his duchy, borrowed forty thousand livres from his mistress, Adrienne Lecouvreur. Having lost the campaign and the money, he returned to Paris and became the darling of the aristocratic ladies, especially the Duchess de Bouillon. See chapter on "History Plays" for details on this story.

37. Adrienne Lecouvreur (1690 - 1730) was the greatest French actress of the eighteenth century. Because she had worked in the theater and could not be buried in consecrated ground, she was buried by night at a private house, 109 Rue de Bourgogne. Another version says her body was wrapped in a sheet and thrown into the Seine. The many romantic stories of her life, and Voltaire's eulogistic poem on her death combined to make her memory revered in France.

38. Matthews, p. 97.

39. Colin Duckworth, "Eugène Scribe and Gérard de Nerval: 'Celui qui tient la corde nous étrangle,' " *Modern Language Review*, 60, 32 - 40.

40. *North American Review*, pp. 327 - 30.

Chapter Two

1. Brander Matthews, *French Dramatists of the Nineteenth Century* (New York: Scribner's, 1881), p. 104.
2. Quoted in Eugene Scribe, *Oeuvres complètes* (Paris: E. Dentu, 1874), I, i, 3 - 4. Unless otherwise noted, all references to plays are from this edition.
3. Scribe, I, i, 4.
4. Collaborator: Charles Délestre-Poirson (1790 - 1859), later manager of the Gymnase. Presented: Vaudeville, November 4, 1815.
5. Collaborator: Jean - Henri Dupin (1791 - 1887), playwright best known for *Mazeppa*. Presented at Variétés, July 12, 1817.
6. Collaborators: Dupin and Nicholas Brazier (1783 - 1838), well-known lyricist. Presented at Variétés, November 7, 1818.
7. Collaborator: G. Delavigne. Presented at Vaudeville, February 8, 1816.
8. Collaborators: Délestre-Poirson and Marc-Antoine-Madeleine Desaugiers (1792 - 1827), known as the "king of lyricists." At this time he was director of the Vaudeville. Presented at Vaudeville, May 8, 1817.
9. Collaborators: Louis-Emmanuel-Félicité-Charles Mercier (1775 - 1851) known as Charles Dupaty, who wrote popular *opéras-comiques*, and Michel Pichot (1786 - 1828), famous for his tragedy, *Turnus*. Presented at Odéon, April 27, 1824.
10. Collaborator: Dupin. Presented at Vaudeville, July 25, 1816.
11. "Farinelli," Grove's *Dictionary of Music and Musicians*, ed. Eric Blom (New York: Saint Martin's, 1955).
12. Collaborator: Germain Delavigne (1790 - 1868), his former schoolmate. Presented at Vaudeville, September 2, 1811.
13. Scribe, *Les Dervis*, II, i, 26.
14. Collaborator Joseph Xavier Saintine (1798 - 1865), whose poem "Picciola" won him the Legion of Honor. Presented at Variétés, February 10, 1820.
15. Collaborator: G. Delavigne. Presented at Odéon, March 19, 1816. This version has no music, but later, revised and with added songs, it was performed at the Gymnase, June 21, 1822 under the title *Les Nouveaux Jeux de l'amour et du hasard*.
16. Collaborator: Délestre-Poirson. Presented at Gymnase, April 23, 1821.
17. Scribe, *Le Parrain*, I, i, 138 - 39.
18. Collaborator: Jean-Albert Imbert (1786 - 1846), who had a distinguished career in the war ministry. Presented at Vaudeville, April 7, 1817.
19. Scribe, *Le Solliciteur*, II, ii, 279.
20. Collaborator: Jean-François-Alfred Bayard (1796 - 1853), known for

comic detail and lively dialogue in his many vaudevilles. Presented at Gymnase [Théâtre de Madame], June 19, 1828.

21. Collaborator: Madame Friedelle. Presented at Gymnase, June 11, 1825.

22. Collaborator: Anne-Honoré-Joseph Duveyrier, known as Charles Mélesville (1787 - 1865), an outstanding author of vaudevilles. Presented at Porte-Saint-Martin, June 10, 1819.

23. Collaborator: Dupin. Presented at Gymnase, December 3, 1821.

24. Scribe, Michel et Christine, II, viii, 282.

25. Collaborator: Marie-Emmanuel-Guillaume-Marguerite Théaulon de Lambert (1787 - 1841), known simply as Théaulon, poet and playwright. Scribe used the pseudonym, "M. Eugène" and the work was not included in Oeuvres complètes, 1874 - 1885. Presented at Variétés, August 8, 1823.

26. Collaborator: Dupin. Presented at Gymnase, October 17, 1823.

27. Collaborator: Mélesville. Presented at Gymnase, November 20, 1823.

28. Collaborator: Camille de Pillet. Presented at Gymnase, [Théâtre de Madame], July 16, 1825.

29. Collaborator: Pierre-Frederic-Adolphe Carmouche (1797 - 1868), a playwright who had worked with Nodier. Presented at Gymnase, March 13, 1823.

Chapter Three

1. Théophile Gautier, Histoire de l'art dramatique en France depuis vingt-cinq ans (Paris: Librairie Maquin, 1859), II, 48 - 49.

2. No collaborator. Presented at Théâtre Français, December 3, 1827.

3. Scribe, Le Mariage d'argent, I, 1, 313.

4. Collaborator: Charles-Henri-Etienne-Edmond Desnoyers, who took the name Etienne de Biéville when he wrote for the stage. He was later editor of Le Siècle (1856). Presented at Théâtre Français, March 1, 1859.

5. Scribe, Rêves d'amour, I, 9, 10 - 11.

6. No collaborator. Presented at Gymnase, January 4, 1831.

7. Scribe, La Famille Riquebourg, ou le Mariage mal assorti, II, 21, 294.

8. Collaborator: Mélesville. Presented at Théâtre Français, April 21, 1842.

9. Scribe, Oscar, ou le Mari qui trompe sa femme, I, 5, 77.

10. No collaborator. Presented at Théâtre Français, November 29, 1841.

11. Alexandre Dumas, fils, La Dame aux camélias, adapted by Sarah Bernhardt (New York: F. Rullman, 1880), p. 28.

12. Collaborator: Francis Cornu was a successful playwright who often wrote under the name "Francis" and was noted for his melodramas. Presented at Gymnase, December 31, 1833.

13. Collaborator: Charles Potron. Presented at Théâre Français, January 23, 1858.

14. Scribe, *Feu Lionel,* I, 8, 41.

15. Collaborator: Emile de Najac was known for his libretti and the "spirituel" quality of his lyrics. Presented at Vaudeville, December 15, 1859.

16. Scribe, *La Fille de trente ans,* I, 9, 130.

17. Ibid.

18. Ibid.

19. No Collaborator. Presented at Théâtre Français, January 19, 1837.

20. Collaborator: Emile-Ernest-Wilfrid Legouvé (1807 - 1903), an outstanding playwright who worked several times with Scribe, and who had already written successfully for the Théâtre Français, *Médée,* a tragedy for Rachel. Presented at Théâtre de la République, March 29, 1858.

21. *Les Doigts de fée,* I, 8, 295.

22. Ibid.

23. Ibid.

24. Collaborator: Legouvé. Presented at Théâtre Français, March 17, 1851.

25. As recently as 1975, Maurice Valency's translation, *The Queen's Gambit,* has appeared in English.

Chapter Four

1. Sir Philip Sidney, "Defence of Poesy" in *Selected Prose and Poetry,* ed. Robert Kimbrough (New York: Holt, Rinehart and Winston, 1969), p. 116.

2. Dumas's *Three Musketeers,* Rostand's *Cyrano de Bergerac* and Giraudoux's *La Guerre de Troie n'aura pas lieu* are only three of many novels, poems and plays following the pattern.

3. Collaborator: G. Delavigne. Presented at Vaudeville, September 27, 1813.

4. Collaborator: Michel-Nicolas Ballison, Baron de Rougemont (1781 - 1840). He resigned a naval career to write for the theater. A brilliant wit, he wrote over two hundred plays. Presented at Gymnase, June 28, 1828.

5. Scribe, II, 18, 56 - 57.

6. Scribe, II, 18, 97.

7. Collaborator: Alexis de Comberousse. Presented at Gymnase, April 18, 1834.

8. Collaborator: Mélesville. Presented at Gymnase, July 8, 1833. On the same night, Scribe's four-act opera, *Ali-Baba,* also written with Mélesville, with music by Cherubini, was presented at the Opéra.

9. Scribe, II, 25, 327.

10. Collaborator: Legouvé. Presented at Théâtre de la République, April 14, 1840.

11. For her death and subsequent events, see chapter on biography. Whatever the disposal of Lecouvreur's body, it stands in marked contrast to

the treatment accorded her English contemporary, Anne Oldfield, who also died in 1730. She was buried in Westminister Abbey with all honors.

12. Ernst Legouvé describes the writing of this scene in his letters.

13. Presented at Gymnase, March 26, 1836.

14. Scribe, II, 28, 30.

15. Collaborator: Paul Duport (1798 - 1866), a brilliant scholar known for his essays on Shakespeare. Presented at Gymnase, September 12, 1833.

16. According to most histories, insanity was suspected.

17. Presented at Théâtre Français, November 14, 1833.

18. Scribe, I, 2, 339.

19. Collaborator: Dupin. Presented at Gymnase, January 14, 1847.

20. Presented at Théâtre Français, October 14, 1850.

21. Scribe, I, 6, 403.

22. Scribe, I, 6, 303.

23. Collaborator: Mélesville. Presented at Gymnase, June 1, 1829.

24. Actually, Gage had eleven children, but the others are not mentioned in the play.

25. The idea of children, particularly girls, being carried off by gypsies was by no means original and is a common romantic theme developed later in Michael Balfe's *The Bohemian Girl* (1843), produced in Paris as *La Bohémienne* (1849). Balfe's librettist, Saint-George, was one of Scribe's collaborators. The theme has certain advantages in its link with the Cinderella motif, with the heroine taking her rightful place in society with magical ease. Bathilde's choice is more rational than the fairy tale or the opera.

26. Presented at Théâtre Français, September 29, 1842.

27. Presented at Gymnase, May 16, 1831.

28. Anne Hyde, James's first wife referred to in the script, died in 1671, long before the time of the play, and the affair between James and Arabella Churchill ended at least ten years before he became king. Curiously, this is the only one of Scribe's historical plays to depart so radically from known facts.

29. Presented at Théâtre Français, November 17, 1840.

30. His name was actually Samuel. No reason is given for the "Arthur" of the script.

31. As recently as April 1976, the Comédie-Française produced a successful revival.

32. Collaborator: Bayard. Presented at Gymnase, October 5, 1836.

33. Presented at Théâtre Français, December 27, 1834.

34. Percy Bysshe Shelley, "A Defence of Poetry" in *The Norton Anthology of English Literature*, II (New York: W. W. Norton, 1974), p. 623.

Chapter Five

1. See Marilyn Lamond, "Notes on Scribe's One-Act *Comédies-Vaudevilles* in Spain 1820 - 1850" *Romance Notes* (Univ. of North Carolina) II, 84 - 93.
2. See John Russell Taylor, *The Rise and Fall of the Well-Made Play* (New York: Hill & Wang, 1969).
3. See Stephen Wischhusen, *The Hour of One* (London: Gordon Fraser, 1975).
4. Taylor, p. 36.
5. Taylor, p. 65.
6. Stephen S. Stanton, "Shaw's Debt to Scribe," *PMLA*, LXXVI (December, 1961), 575 - 85.
7. Ronald Grimsley, *Soren Kierkegaard and French Literature* (Cardiff: Univ. of Wales, 1966), pp. 112 - 29.
8. Arthur Aumont and Edgar Collin, *Den danske Nationaltheater 1748 - 1884*, 3 vols. 1896 - 1899.
9. Colin Duckworth, "Pour le centenaire d'Eugène Scribe." *Theatre Research*, III, 43 - 49.
10. Hans-George Ruprecht, *Theaterpublikum und Textauffassung.* Bern: Lang, 1976.

Chapter Six

1. Quoted in the introduction to the libretto accompanying the private recording of the opera's revival in 1960 at La Scala.
2. By Charles Nodier.
3. Scribe, II, vi, 309.
4. Ibid.
5. *Ruddigore*, Act II, Trio: Robin, Despard and Margaret.
6. Scribe, *Opéras*, II, v, 68.
7. *L'Artiste* (1834), p. 222.
8. Scribe, I, i, 3.
9. Scribe, II, i, 30.
10. Scribe, IV, v, 65.
11. Two arias and some recitative were composed by Berlioz. The manuscripts have been preserved and the music has actually been performed in recent times.
12. Act II, ii, *Opéras*, VI, 26 - 27.

Selected Bibliography

PRIMARY SOURCES

Oeuvres complètes. Paris: Dentu, n.d. 75 Volumes. This is the first of the almost-complete works. Earlier editions termed *oeuvres complètes* were only partial editions.

Oeuvres complètes, nouvelle édition. Paris: Dentu, 1874 - 1885. 76 volumes, Series 1: comédies, drames, 9 volumes; series 2: comédies, vaudevilles, 33 volumes; series 3: opéras, ballets, 6 volumes; series 4: opéras-comiques, 20 volumes; series 5: proverbes, nouvelles, romans, 8 volumes. A sixth series was projected (oeuvres diverses et inédites), but was never published. This edition has been used for reference in the text. It is available in microfilm edition: Brookhaven Press, La Crosse, Wisconsin.

Théâtre choisi d'Eugène Scribe. Paris: Delagrave, 1911. Contains six plays: *L'Ours et le pacha, Le Diplomate, Bertrand et Raton, La Cameraderie, Le Verre d'eau,* and *Adrienne Lecouvreur.* Four subsequent reeditions appeared: 1918, 1923, 1929, and 1932.

Three Centuries of French Drama. Louisville: Falls City Press, 1959 - . This is a microfiche edition of French plays. It contains numerous plays by Scribe.

1. Individual Plays

Only twentieth-century editions have been noted. In general, most of the plays appeared first at the time of performance in individual pamphlet editions, then later in various collections such as the popular illustrated theater publications, then in various collections such as series covering the repertory of a given theater (such as the Théâtre de Madame).

Adrienne Lecouvreur.
Paris: Levy, 1903.
London, 1907. (School Text)
Paris: Calmann-Levy, 1908.
New York: Oxford, 1917. (School Text)
English Translation: New York, 1942.
Bataille de dames.
Paris: Calmann-Levy, 1905.
New York: Heath, 1908. (School Text)

Boston: Heath, 1911. (School Text)
Ann Arbor, 1923.
New York: American Book Company, 1923. (School Text)
Bertrand et Raton.
    New York: Jenkins, 1902.
    Paris: La Renaissance de Livre, 1918.
    Paris: Hatier, 193 - (?)
La Cameraderie.
    Boston: Allyn and Bacon, 1920.
Les Doigts de fée.
    Paris: Calmann-Levy, 1907.
    New York and Strasbourg, 1913.
The Queen's Gambit.
    New York: Samuel French, 1955.
Une Chaîne.
    London: Hachette, 1912.
Le Verre d'eau.
    Boston: Heath, 1900, 1916. (School Text)
    Cambridge, 1900. (School Text)
    New York: Jenkins, 1904. (School Text)
    New York and Strasbourg, 1911.
    Paris: Levy, 1911.
    English Translation: London, 1950.
    See also the translation published by Stanton, below.

SECONDARY SOURCES

ALLARD, LOUIS. *La Comédie de moeurs en France au dix-neuvième siècle.* Paris: Hachette, 1933. 2 volumes. One of the basic works. Volume II covers Scribe.

ARVIN, NEIL. *Eugène Scribe and the French Theatre (1815 - 1860).* Cambridge: Harvard, 1924. The only comprehensive study in English centering on Scribe.

CARDWELL, WALTER. *The Dramaturgy of Eugène Scribe.* Diss. *DSA*, XXXII (1971), 1505A (Yale). An interesting study from the technical point of view: use of props, questions of staging, dramatic construction.

Comédie française. (Periodical). No. 48, April, 1976. A special number of the magazine on the occasion of the revival of *Le Verre d'eau.* Articles on Scribe and the play.

LAMM, MARTIN. *Modern Drama.* New York: Philosophical Library, 1953. Places Scribe in the history of drama.

LECIGNE, C. *Scribe et son théâtre.* Arras, 1906. A good example of the body of criticism tending to denigrate Scribe.

LEGOUVÉ, ERNEST. *Eugène Scribe.* Paris: Dentu, 1874. A sympathetic view of Scribe by his contemporary, his good friend and collaborator.

MATTHEWS, J. BRANDER. "Eugène Scribe" in *French Dramatists of the 19th Century*. London: Remington, 1882. And old, but authoritative study by one of the classic historians of the theater.

MIRECOURT, EUGÈNE DE. *Scribe*. Paris, 1853. Also published in *Les Contemporains* (a series of 140 pamphlets) Paris, 1867 - . Another contemporary and friendly view of the playwright.

ROLLAND, J. *Les Comédies historiques et politiques d'Eugène Scribe*. Paris: Bibliothèque des Hautes-Etudes Sociales, 1933. A serious look at Scribe's work, focussing particularly on the sociological aspects: Scribe as a reflection of Society.

STANTON, STEVEN. *Camille and Other Plays*. New York: Hill and Wang, 1957. The introduction places Scribe in the history of drama. *The Glass of Water* is one of the plays by various authors presented in English translation in this anthology.

———. "Shaw's Debt to Scribe." *PMLA*, LXXVI (December, 1961). A detailed study of perhaps the most important Scribe influence.

TAYLOR, JOHN RUSSELL. *The Rise and the Fall of the Well-Made Play*. New York: Hill and Wang, 1967. Studies the history of the English playwrights who followed in the footsteps of Scribe.

VALENCY, MAURICE. *The Flower and the Castle, an Introduction to the Modern Drama*. New York: MacMillan, 1963. Contains a general evaluation of Scribe in context. Valency is a translator (*The Queen's Gambit*, cited above, is his translation.)

Index

Académie-Française, 11, 26, 32
Acton, Lord, 87
Adam, Adolphe, 23
Addison, Joseph, 114
Adriana Lecouvreur (Cilea), 96
Africaine, L' (Meyerbeer), 33, 150, 152
Ali-Baba (Cherubini), 163
Andromaque (Racine), 33
Anne, Queen, 106
Antony (Dumas), 155
Armida (Rossini), 160
Arnault, Vincent-Antoine, 11, 26, 27, 159
Art poétique (Verlaine), 130
Auber, Daniel-François-Esprit, 8, 123, 125, 126
Audébrand, Philippe, 32, 33
Augier, Emile, 34
Aumer, M., 27
Axël (Villiers), 155

Balfe, Michael, 164
Ballison, M.-N., 163
Ballo in maschera, Un (Verdi), 147
Balzac, Honoré de, 111, 112
Bartram (Maturin), 134
Bastien und Bastienne (Mozart), 132
Bayard, Jean-François-Alfred, 30, 159, 161, 164
Beaumarchais, Pierre-Augustin, 22
Becque, Henri, 113, 128
Bellini, Vincenzo, 23
Berlioz, Hector, 145, 148, 165
Bernhardt, Sarah, 32, 35, 112
Béranger, Pierre Jean de, 28
Bernadotte, Jean-Baptiste-Jules, 159
Berry, Duchess de, 7, 23
Beyle, Marie-Henri. *See* Stendhal
Biéville, Etienne de, 33, 162
Biollay, M., 28

Bizet, Georges, 126
Bloody Nun, The. See Nonne sanglante, La
Bohemian Girl, The (Balfe), 164
Bohémienne, La (Balfe). *See Bohemian Girl, The*
Boieldieu, Adrien, 45, 125, 127
Bonaparte, Napoleon, 11, 61
Bonnet, Louis-Ferdinand, 12, 159
Bonynge, Richard, 123
Bouillon, Duchess de, 31
Brazier, Nicholas, 16, 161
Bretón de los Herreros, 114, 115
Brieux, Eugène de, 34
Brunet, Jean-Joseph (Mira), 16

Cadalso, José, 114
Camberousse, Alexis de, 163
Candida (Shaw), 118
Captain Brassbound's Conversion (Shaw), 118
Carmen (Bizet), 126
Carmouche, Pierre-Frédéric, 19, 162
Cartas marruescas (Cadalso), 114
Castle Spectre (Lewis), 116
Catherine II of Russia, 97
Cavalleria Rusticana (Mascagni), 137
Cerfberr, Alphonse, 17
Charles V, 101
Chateaubriand, F. R. de., 139
Chatte merveilleuse, La (Désaugiers), 22
Chatterton (Vigny), 111
Cherubini, Luigi, 23, 125, 163
Christian VII (Denmark), 98
Chronicles of the Time of Charles IX (Vigny), 139
Churchill, Arabella, 104
Churchill, James, 164
Cid, Le (Corneille), 33
Clapisson, A.L., 125

Coll, D.-G.-F., 114
Cologno, Francesco, 114
Comédie Française, 7, 12, 17, 19, 25, 27
Comédie humaine (Balzac), 112
Comte Ory (Rossini), 126, 131
Conjuración de Venecia (García Gutiérrez), 114
Coquelin, Benoît-Constant, 35
Corbeaux, Les (Becque), 113, 128
Corneille, Pierre, 7, 125
Cornu, Francis, 25, 162
Cromwell (Hugo), 139
Cyrano de Bergerac (Rostand), 163

Dame blanche, La (Boieldieu), 45, 122, 126, 127
Dame aux camélias, La (Dumas), 160, 162
Delavigne, Casimir, 14, 24
Delavigne, Germain, 12, 13, 14, 24, 161
Délestre-Poirson, Charles, 13, 14, 15, 16, 17, 20, 161
Désaugiers, Marc-Antoine-Madeleine, 22, 161
Desnoyers, C.-H., -E.-E. See Biéville
Destouches, Philippe-Néricault, 26
Devil's Disciple, The (Shaw), 118
Devin du village, Le (Rousseau), 132
Diderot, Denis, 112
Don Giovanni (Mozart), 132
Donizetti, Gaetano, 125, 126
Dubois, Abbé, 92
Dumas, Alexandre, père, 112, 154, 155, 163
Dumas, Alexandre, fils, 30, 35, 160, 162
Dupaty. See Mercier
Dupin, Andre-Marie-Jean-Jacques, 12
Dupin, Jean-Henri, 13, 14, 15, 16, 18, 161, 162, 164
Duport, Paul, 164
Duveyrier, Joseph. See Mélesville

Ein' feste Burg (Luther), 142
Elizabeth, Queen of England (Rossini), 140
Ellsler, Fanny, 27, 160

Falstaff (Verdi), 133, 149
Farinelli, 161
Faust (Gounod), 137, 145
Favorita, La (Donizetti), 126
Fay, Léontine, 19
Feuillet, Octave, 40
Feydeau, Georges, 113, 156
Fields, W. C., 115
Figaro, Le, 25, 33
Fitch, Clyde, 117
Flaubert, Gustave, 154, 155
François I, 101
Frankenstein (Milner), 116
Freischütz, Der (Weber), 126
Friedelle, Madame, 20, 21, 162

Gage, Lord, 103
Gaîté, Théâtre de la, 17
García Gutiérrez, 114
Gautier, Théophile, 30, 63, 122, 162
Gazette de Paris, La, 32, 33
Genius of Christianity (Chateaubriand), 139
Gentil, Michel-Joseph, 22
George I, 107
George II, 108
Gil, Isidoro, 114
Gil de Zarate, 114
Gilbert, W. S., 133
Giraudoux, Jean, 163
Girl with the Green Eyes, The (Fitch), 117
Glass of Water (Robertson), 115
Glass of White Beer, 120
Goethe, Johann Wolfgang von, 100
Gounod, Charles, 23, 125, 134, 145, 148
Grundy, Sidney, 115
Guerre de Troie n'aura pas lieu, La (Giraudoux), 163
Guyot, Pierre-François, 20
Gymnase, Théâtre du, 17, 19, 20, 23, 25, 31

Halévy, Jacques, 8, 23, 125, 126, 136, 139
Hartzenbusch, J. E., 114
Heine, Heinrich, 39
Henri III and his Court (Dumas), 155

Héreau, Philippe, 32
Hernani (Hugo), 111, 155
Hugo, Victor, 111, 112, 130, 139, 152, 155
Huguenots, Les (Meyerbeer), 126, 139
Hunchback of Notre Dame, The (Hugo). *See Notre Dame de Paris*
Hyde, Anne, 164

Ibsen, Henrik, 7, 29, 118-19, 121
Imbert, J.-A., 161
Italian, The (Radcliffe), 134

Jones, Henry Arthur, 116
Juive, La (Halévy), 126, 136, 139

Kierkegaard, Sören, 119-20

La Roserie, 17
Labrunie, Gérard. *See* Gérard de Nerval
Ladies' Battle, The (Robertson), 115
Lady in White, The. See La Dame blanche
Larra, Mariano José de, 114
Lecouvreur, Adrienne, 94, 160, 163
Legouvé, Emile, 31, 123, 163, 164
Léo Burkhardt (Nerval), 154
Lewis, Matthew Gregory, 134, 145
Lino Zayati, Genaro, 114
Louis XV, 12, 26
Louis-Philippe, 23, 92
Lucrèce (Poinsard), 33
Luther, Martin, 142

Maine, Duchesse du, 92
Man and Superman (Shaw), 118
Maquet, Auguste, 33
Marguerite de Navarre, 101, 140
Marie Antoinette, 89
Marlborough, John, Duke of, 29
Marlborough family, 106
Mars, Mademoiselle (Anne-Françoise-Hippolyte Boutet), 19
Matthews, Brander, 32
Maturin, Charles, 134
Médée (Legouvé), 31, 163
Mélesville, Charles (Joseph

Duveyrier), 17, 19, 21, 159, 162, 164
Mercier, L.-E.-F.-C., 161
Meyerbeer, Giacomo, 23, 24, 123, 126, 134, 136, 139, 143, 145, 150, 152
Misanthrope, Le (Molière), 15
Misérables, Les (Hugo), 112
Modjeska, Helena, 32
Molière (Jean-Baptiste Poquelin), 12, 26, 34, 35, 115, 119, 132, 156
Monk, The (Lewis), 134, 145
Monténégrins, Les (Nerval), 154
Moratín, Leandro, 113
Moreau, Charles, 17
Moreau, Jean-Victor, 12, 159
Mozart, Wolfgang Amadeus, 132, 133
Muette de Portici, La (Auber), 126
Musset, Alfred de, 111, 112
Mysteries of Udolpho, The (Radcliffe), 129, 134

Najac, Emile de, 163
Napoleon, 98, 159
Nerval, Gérard de, 32, 111, 112, 154
Nivelle de La Chaussée, 26
Nodier, Charles, 58, 59, 128, 134, 162, 165
Nonne sanglante, La (Gounod), 134, 145
Notre Dame de Paris (Hugo), 112

Odéon, Théâtre de l', 17, 45
Offenbach, Jacques, 125
Oldfield, Anne, 164
Opéra, Théâtre de l', 17, 31
Opéra-Comique, 17, 25, 31
Ossian, 128

Parisienne, La (Becque), 113
Paul and Virginia (Saint-Pierre), 152
Peral, Juan del, 114
Perlet, Adrien, 56
Phèdre (Racine), 94
Philip V, 47
Philippe, Gérard, 112
Philippe d'Orléans, 92
Pichot, Michel, 161
Pillet, Camille de, 162
Pinero, Arthur Wing, 116, 119

Pirandello, Luigi, 100
Planche, Gustave, 24
Poliuto (Les Martyrs) (Donizetti), 125
Polyeucte (Corneille), 125
Prophète, Le (Meyerbeer), 33, 115, 123, 126, 143
Poquelin, Jean-Baptiste. See Molière
Potemkin, Prince, 97
Potier, Charles, 13, 51
Potron, Charles, 162

Rachel (Elizabeth Félix), 31, 32, 163
Racine, Jean-Baptiste, 26, 34, 35, 156
Radcliffe, Ann, 129, 134
Ramón de Arriola, 114
Ramón de Navarrete, 114
Rasputin, 98
Regency (of Philippe d'Orléans), 92
Rigoletto (Verdi), 147
Ristori, Adelaide, 31
Robert le Diable (Meyerbeer), 23, 24, 126, 134
Robertson, Tom, 115
Romea, Julián, 114
Romeo and Juliet (Berlioz), 148
Romeo and Juliet (Shakespeare), 148
Roméo et Juliette (Gounod), 145, 148
Rossini, Gioacchino, 23, 125, 126, 131, 140
Rostand, Edmond, 163
Rougemont, Baron de. See Ballison
Rousseau, Jean-Jacques, 132
Ruddigore (Gilbert and Sullivan), 133, 165
Ruy Blas (Hugo), 111, 155

Saint-Georges, Jules-Henri de, 18, 19, 164
Saint-Pierre, Barnardin, 152
Saint-Saëns, Camille, 145
Saintine, Xavier, 20, 161
Samson and Delilah (Saint-Saëns), 145
Sarcey, Francisque, 29, 36
Sardou, Victorien, 29, 34
Saxe, Maurice de, 94, 160
Schlegel, Auguste Wilhelm von, 15
Scribe, Augustin-Eugène, Académie-Française, 26-27; American history plays, 103-104; Ballets, 123-24;

Characters, 38-39, 62; Comédie-Française, 19-21; Dramatic success, 14-16; Early years, 11-13; English history plays, 104-109; European history plays, 96-103; Farces, 47-54; First plays, 13-14; French history plays, 88-96; Influence on English drama, 115-18; Influence on European drama, 118-21; Influence on French drama, 111-13; Influence on Spanish drama, 113-15; Italian operas, 147-51; July Revolution, 21-23; Language, 39-40; Last years, 30-34; Literary-theatrical satires, 43-47; Marriage, 27-30; Middle years, 23-26; Operas, 124-47; Popularity, 16-17; Realism, 62-63; Sentimental plays, 55-59; Serious plays, 54; Social concerns, 61-63; Social plays, 84-85; Structural innovations, 36-38; Subjects, 40; Technique, 17-19, 86-88, 109-10, 122-23, 152-53; Topical works, 41-43

WORKS:
Abuelito, El (Le Bon Papa), 114
Adrienne Lecouvreur, 31, 32, 94, 116, 117, 141
Amante prestado, El (Zoé), 115
Ambitieux, L', 25, 29, 108
Auberge, ou les Brigands sans le savoir, L', 13, 19
Avant, pendant et après, 89
Bachelier de Salamanque, Le, 14
Bal Masqué, Le, 147
Barbanéra, ou la Nuit des noces, 14
Bataille de dames, 32, 83-84, 101
Bertrand et Raton, 25, 29, 98
Bohémienne, La, 103
Bon Papa, Le, 114
Boulevard Bonne-Nouvelle, Le, 17
Café des Variétés, La, 16
Calomnie, La, 29
Camaraderie, La, 27, 77-80
Camélias, 160
Camilla, 160
Carlo Broschi, 30, 45, 46-47

Chambre à coucher, La, 13
Chanoinesse, La, 72-73
Charivari, La, 32, 33
Chut!, 96
Combat des montagnes, Le, 15, 41-42, 47
Comtesse de Troun, La, 14
Contes de la reine de Navarre, 101
Dame de Pique, La, 33
Dervis, Les, 13, 47-48
Dix ans de la vie d'une femme, 24, 69-70, 72, 81
Doigts de fée, Les, 80-82, 163
Écarté, 19
Empiriques d'autrefois, Les, 52-53
Famille Riquebourg, ou le Mariage mal assorti, La, 68-69, 162
Farinelli, ou la Pièce de circonstance, 46-47
Favorite, La (vaudeville), 105
Feu Lionel, 73-75, 76, 163
Fille de trente ans, La, 75-77, 163
Filleul d'Amadis, ou les Amours d'une fée, 30
Fils de Cromwel, 104, 108
Fleurette, 30
Flore et Zéphire, 15, 43-44, 46
Florinda, 29
Frères invisibles, Les, 54
Foyer du Gymnase, Le, 159
Glass of Water, See Le Verre d'eau
Hôtel des quatre nations, L', 16, 42-43
Irlandais, L', 29
Kiosque, Le, 31
Koulikan, 13, 31
Leicester, 45
Maître Jean, 100
Manie des places, ou la Folie du siècle, La, 51-52
Marco Spada, 123
Mariage d'argent, Le, 21, 64-67, 73, 162
Mariage de raison, Le, 21
Mauvais sujet, Le, 58
Michel et Christine, 18, 55-56, 58, 162
Mort et le Bûcheron, La, 14
Moulin de Javelle, La, 92
Neige, La, 45
No más muchachas (*Le Vieux Garçon*

et la petite fille), 114-15
Nouveaux jeux de l'amour et du hasard, Les, 161
Oscar, ou le Mari qui trompe sa femme, 29, 70-71, 162
Ours et le Pacha, L', 48-49, 53
Parrain, Le, 50
Perruque et la redingote, La, 14
Philtre, Le, 23
Piquillo Alliagra, 30
Pompe funèbre, La, 14
Premières amours, Les, 114
Prétendu par hasard, ou l'Occasion fait le larron, Le, 13
Primeros amores, Los (*Les Premières amours*), 114
Protectrice et le ministre, La, 23
Queen's Gambit, 163
Retour, ou la Suite de Michel et Christine, Le, 57
Rêves d'amour, 67-68, 162
Rodolphe, ou Frère et soeur, 57
Salvoisy, 91
Seconde année, La, 114
Segundo año, El (*La Seconde année*), 114
Sir Hugues de Guilfort, 107
Solliciteur, ou l'Art d'obtenir des places, Le, 15, 27, 50-51, 161
Somnambule, La, 27
Stanislas, 56, 57
Tempête, La, 29
Thibault, Comte de Champagne, 14, 58
Thomas le chanceux, ou les trois bossus, 14
Trilby, ou le Lutin d'Argail, 58-59
Trois Genres, Les, 45-46
Un paseo a Bedlam (*Une Visite à Bedlam*), 114
Un trait de Paul Ier, 98
Une chaîne, 29, 71-72
Une chainoinesse, 25
Une faute, 159
Une nuit de la Garde nationale, 14, 15, 41
Une visite à Bedlam, 16, 114
Valérie, 19
Valet de son rival, Le, 49-50, 53

Verre d'eau, Le, 29, 108, 116, 120, 155, 156
Vieux chateau, Le, 32
Vieux Garçon et la petite fille, Le, 114–15
Volière, La, 27
Wallace, ou la Barrière Mont-Parnasse, 44–45, 46
Yelva, 31
Zoé, 115

Scribe, Madame (mother), 12
Scribe, Madame (wife), 28
Second Mrs. Tanqueray (Pinero), 116–117
Shakespeare, William, 111, 119, 148, 164
Shaw, George Bernard, 111, 113, 118
Shelley, Percy Bysshe, 110
Sicilian Vespers. See *Vêpres siciliennes, Les*
Sidney, Sir Philip, 88
Siècle, Le, 30, 33, 162
Société des Auteurs et Compositeurs Dramatiques, 22, 23, 33
Spectator, The (Addison and Steele), 114
Steele, Richard, 114
Stendhal, 154
Strnsée, Johann Friedrich von, 25, 98, 160
Sullivan, Sir Arthur, 133

Tancredi (Rossini), 140
Tartuffe (Molière), 33
Théâtre de Bruxelles, 17
Théâtre de Madame. See Gymnase
Théâtre de la Pigalle, 17
Théâtre de la République, 31
Théâtre des Nouveautés, 17

Théâtre en liberté (Hugo), 112
Theatre Royal (Hague), 32
Théaulon de ambert, M.-E.-G.-M., 162
Thomas, Ambroise, 23, 125
Three Musketeers, The (Dumas), 163
Traviata, La (Verdi), 137, 147
Trelawney of the Wells (Pinero), 116–17, 119
Trilby (Nodier), 128
Trovatore, Il (Verdi), 147
Truth (Fitch), 117

Valency, Maurice, 163
Vampire (Planché), 116
Varner, François-Antoine, 21
Variétés, Théâtre des, 13, 15, 17, 22
Vasco da Gama, 150
Vaudeville, Théâtre de, 13, 14, 17, 22, 51
Ventura de la Vega, 114
Vêpres Siciliennes, Les (Verdi), 33, 147
Verlaine, Paul, 130
Verdi, Giuseppe, 8, 23, 125, 133, 147
Vespri siciliani. See *Vêpres siciliennes, Les*
Viaggio a Reims, Il (Rossini), 134
Vigny, Alfred de, 111, 139
Villeneuve, Théodore-Ferdinand Vallon de, 26
Villiers de l'Isle Adam, Auguste, Comte de, 155
Voltaire, François-Marie Arouet de, 26, 160

Walpole, Robert, 25, 108
Weber, Karl Maria von, 125, 126
William Tell (Rossini), 140

Zola, Emile, 112